LEADERSHIP REFRAMED

How Great Leaders Invest in People to
Build Autonomous Excellence

Michael A. Bruggeman

INVESTED
LEADERSHIP

Published by Invested Leadership, LLC.

ISBN: 979-8-9945724-4-3

DISCLAIMER
This book is intended for informational and educational purposes only. The author is not engaged in rendering legal, medical, financial, or professional advice. The content reflects the author's personal experience, perspective, and interpretation of leadership principles. Readers should consult appropriate professionals before making decisions based on the information contained in this book.

This book contains a brief, non-graphic reference to suicide. I include it with care, and I recognize it may be heavy for some readers. If you'd like to skip that section, you can do so without losing the main thread of the book. A resource section is included in the back matter for anyone who may need support or who wants to help someone else.

CASES, STORIES, AND EXAMPLES
The stories, case studies, and examples in this book are provided for illustrative purposes. Names, roles, organizations, and identifying details have been changed to protect privacy. Any resemblance to actual persons, living or deceased, or to actual organizations or events is coincidental unless otherwise stated.

TRADEMARKS AND ATTRIBUTIONS
All company names, product names, logos, and trademarks referenced in this book are the property of their respective owners and are referenced in the back of the book.

PERMISSIONS
I've made every effort to ensure that all material referenced or quoted in this book complies with applicable fair-use standards.

Table of Contents

Acknowledgements

This book exists because I've been surrounded by people who invested in me long before I understood the power of investment.

First, to my wife, Kristin—thank you for being my anchor. You've carried more than your share of the unseen weight: late nights, long seasons, big risks, and the emotional spill-over that leadership can create at home. You've believed in the work, challenged the parts that needed refining, and reminded me—again and again—what actually matters. I'm better because of you.

To my kids, Emma and Logan—thank you for your patience and your joy. You've taught me that love isn't a concept; it's a practice. If this book helps leaders build healthier cultures, it's because you've kept my heart tethered to what leadership is really for: people.

To the leaders who took a chance on me early—thank you for the opportunities, the honest feedback, and the kind of trust that raises the standard. You didn't just teach me how to execute. You taught me how to think.

To the teams I've had the privilege to lead—this book is, in many ways, your story. You showed me what ownership looks like when it's real. Many of the best lessons in these pages came from watching you do the work with excellence—and watching you do it with passion.

And to you, the reader, thank you for being the kind of leader who's willing to look in the mirror. If you're here, it means you're not satisfied with being the bottleneck. You're choosing the harder path: building people, building culture, and building something that compounds.

If this book does its job, you'll close it with one clear conviction:

The best leaders don't try to get more out of people. They invest more in them.

—Michael A. Bruggeman

Introduction

If you and I were sitting in a coffee shop right now—the kind with warm lighting, soft jazz, and a barista who somehow remembers everyone's favorite drink—I'd ease into this conversation the same way I ease into most important truths: slowly, honestly, and with just enough self-awareness to admit where I got it wrong.

There's something about a coffee shop that makes honesty feel less like a performance and more like a shared breath. Maybe it's the hum of people thinking their own thoughts, or the way time stretches just enough for reflection to feel possible. Whatever it is, this is the place where I'd feel comfortable telling you something I didn't admit early in my career:

I thought leadership was mostly about being in charge.

Not in an egotistical way—at least that's what I told myself. It was subtler than that. I believed leadership meant having the answers, projecting certainty, speaking with the confidence that made people nod even when they weren't fully sure why. I imagined leadership as a performance: clipboard in hand, decisive tone, and the subtle illusion that responsibility rested on your shoulders because you were somehow more prepared, more capable, or more informed.

But leadership has a way of exposing whatever illusions you bring into it.

That truth didn't arrive in a single dramatic moment. It surfaced gradually—in the conversations where I spoke too quickly and understood too slowly, in the late evenings replaying decisions that hadn't landed the way I expected, and in the moments where the people I led weren't responding to my confidence at all. They were responding to my attention… or my absence.

Somewhere along the way, I realized leadership wasn't about speaking louder. It was about listening longer than I was comfortable. Asking questions before offering answers and seeing people as human beings with stories, fears, strengths, and brilliance long before I needed anything from them.

Leadership wasn't a performance.

It was a relationship.

And relationships aren't built in speeches. They're built in steady, unglamorous moments of presence.

When that truth finally settled in, leadership stopped feeling like a costume I had to keep adjusting. It began to feel like a posture I could grow into—slowly, intentionally, almost without forcing it. It became less about being impressive and more about being invested.

That's when the clearest leadership truth I've ever encountered surfaced with enough force that I couldn't ignore it:

Leaders exist to invest and empower others to be autonomously excellent.

Everything in this book flows from that simple, disruptive idea.

Not excellence born of pressure or perfectionism, but the kind that grows naturally when people feel seen, supported, trusted, and given space to rise. Not autonomy as chaos, but autonomy grounded in clarity. Not empowerment as a buzzword, but as a steady belief in someone's capacity long before they see it themselves.

This book isn't a corporate manifesto or a collection of leadership hacks. It's closer to two humans sitting with chipped mugs, trading stories about what leadership actually feels like—not in theory, but in the moments where it's inconvenient, unplanned, or transformative without announcing itself. The moments that shape people far more than polished strategies ever could.

Because leadership doesn't live in mission statements, it lives in the pause before reacting. In the courage to admit when you're wrong. In a conversation in which someone finally feels safe enough to tell you the truth. In the moment you loosen your grip instead of tightening it.

In short, leadership lives in people.

If you're reading this, you're probably someone who wants to lead in a way that builds people rather than burns them out. You want your leadership to matter—not because of your title, but because of your impact. You want to walk into a room and make it a little lighter, not a little tenser. You want to build something that lasts.

If so, you're in the right place.

Before we go any further, though, I want to offer something I wish someone had handed me when I first stepped into leadership: permission to be unfinished.

Most leadership books imply that leaders are supposed to arrive somewhere—that with enough discipline, enough systems, and enough color-coded planners, you'll eventually reach a place where certainty replaces doubt and clarity flows effortlessly. Real leadership doesn't work like that. Not for me. Not for anyone I've ever met.

Leaders aren't finished products. They're works in progress who grow—not because they're inadequate, but because the people they lead deserve a version of them that keeps becoming wiser, steadier, and more attuned.

That growth rarely comes in grand epiphanies. It comes through the slow accumulation of small, human moments—the ones that make you pause and think, "Alright. I can do better next time."

Some of the most formative leadership moments of my career didn't happen in boardrooms. They happened in hallways, exam rooms, supply closets, and late-night phone calls—moments where someone trusted me with frustration or fear, and I had to decide whether I'd meet them with presence or with pretense.

People don't follow flawless leaders. They follow human ones.

They don't need you to be impressive—just invested. They need your attention, your curiosity, and your willingness to believe in them without keeping score.

That posture is the heartbeat of the Invested Leadership platform—and this book, Leadership Reframed, is where I lay out the framework (to prevent confusion, I will sometimes refer to it as reframed leadership, too). A way of leading that centers on people, prioritizes development, and understands that excellence is cultivated with people, not extracted from them.

As we move forward, my goal isn't to hand you a checklist. It's to offer a lens—one that helps you see why certain leadership moments work and why others quietly fail. Leadership becomes far more navigable when you understand the patterns beneath the surface.

You'll see one truth repeated throughout these pages:

People don't quit jobs.

They quit leaders.

And people don't stay for paychecks—they stay for belief: in themselves, in the work, and in the sense that they matter.

When a leader invests in someone—not as a resource, but as a person—it changes how that person shows up, thinks, and cares. And over time, the culture around them shifts.

This framework isn't about directing traffic. It's about clearing pathways. Less about holding authority and more about holding space. Less about being the smartest person in the room and more about helping others discover their own capacity.

And here's the paradox that sits at the heart of this book:

When you lead like that, people don't follow you because they have to. They follow because they grow in your presence. That is the steady influence of an invested leader.

Not loud. Not showy.

But unmistakable.

So, settle in. Take a breath. Let the noise settle just enough for clarity to surface.

Before we talk about trust, empowerment, autonomy, or excellence, we need to start with something simpler—and far more foundational:

Leadership is not what you control.
It's what you invest in.

And that's where the real work begins.

Part I: The Foundation

Most leadership problems don't start with skill gaps. They start with orientation—what you believe leadership is for. This part answers: **Are you building results, or building people?** You'll shift from measuring leadership by control and output to measuring it by what your leadership produces in others over time: confidence, ownership, initiative, and steadiness under pressure.

Watch for mistaking control for competence, confusing busyness with leadership, and assuming compliance is the same as commitment.

This is the starting point: leadership is not what you control. It's what you invest in.

Chapter 1 – Rethinking Leadership

I didn't set out to rethink leadership. I just kept running into the same uncomfortable question—one that followed me longer than I care to admit.

Why did some people grow under my leadership while others slowly disappeared, even when the numbers looked good?

Early in my career, I did what I'd learned—set direction, make decisions, hold people accountable, keep things moving. Leadership, as I understood it, was largely about momentum—forward progress, visible results, and making sure nothing stalled. If something wasn't working, the fix was usually straightforward: clarify expectations, tighten timelines, increase oversight. And when I'm honest with myself, I mistook control for competence more than once.

On paper, it worked—projects launched and targets were hit. I earned credibility by being decisive and dependable.

From the outside, leadership appeared to be doing exactly what it was supposed to do.

But from the inside, something felt incomplete.

People did what I asked of them, but rarely more than that. They showed up, but not always fully. Meetings were efficient, yet oddly subdued. Feedback sounded agreeable but lacked conviction. And when something went wrong, eyes subtly shifted upward—waiting for my direction rather than taking action. No one was sabotaging the work. No one was disengaged enough to cause alarm. But no one was really owning it either.

That's a harder problem to diagnose.

It's easy to spot failure. It's much harder to recognize leadership that's functional but unfulfilling—effective enough to pass reviews, yet shallow enough to leave potential untouched. For a long time, I assumed that was just the cost of doing business. Not everyone is wired to lead. Not everyone wants more responsibility. Not everyone will be passionate about the work.

Those explanations were convenient. They were also incomplete.

Over time, patterns started to emerge. The same types of people seemed to stall. The same dips in energy occurred after similar decisions. And the same teams that looked solid during calm periods struggled disproportionately when pressure arrived. I could feel the gap between compliance and commitment widening, but I didn't yet have language for what I was seeing.

That question—"why do some people grow and others fade?"—followed me everywhere. Into performance reviews that felt more like scorekeeping than development. Into leadership meetings where alignment was high and ownership was low. Into moments where I realized I had plenty of authority, but far less influence than I assumed.

Eventually, it forced me to confront a harder truth. I had been measuring leadership by what people *produced* rather than by who they were *becoming*.

Once I saw that, I couldn't unsee it. Results suddenly felt like a lagging indicator, not the whole story. What mattered just as much was the confidence people carried into decisions, the initiative they brought into ambiguity, and the courage they showed when something didn't go according to plan. Those qualities weren't random. Leadership shaped them—slowly, in layers.

That's when the idea of leadership as investment began to take shape for me.

Investment reframes everything. It shifts your focus from immediate output to long-term growth. It forces patience where urgency once dominated. It demands belief where control once felt safer. When you invest, you accept that the return won't always be visible right away, and you're okay with that because you believe in what you're building beneath the surface.

That lens changed how I understood my role.

Leadership shifted from my presence in the room to my impact over time. It wasn't about how often I spoke; it was about what lingered after I left, not about how tightly I held decisions, but about how people experienced responsibility when it arose. The question shifted from "What did we get done today?" to "What did this experience build in them?"

That shift exposed something else I hadn't fully appreciated before.

Every leader creates an emotional environment. Whether intentional or not, leadership sets the tone for how people experience their work. Some environments invite curiosity and ownership. Others discourage risk and initiative without ever saying so. Some rooms feel steady even under pressure. Others feel brittle the moment things get uncomfortable. That atmosphere isn't accidental—it's constructed through everyday interactions, reactions, and priorities.

And here's the uncomfortable part: leaders are often the last to feel the environment they create.

People adapt, read cues, and adjust their behavior. Over time, they either expand or contract in response to what leadership consistently rewards or discourages. You don't have to announce distrust or danger for people to feel it—and shut down. The signals are subtler than that, but they're remarkably effective.

Once I understood leadership as stewardship, things became clearer.

You don't own people's talent. You're entrusted with it for a season. What you do with that trust—how you invest your attention, your belief, your willingness to let others grow—shapes outcomes that last far longer than your tenure. Leadership, at its best, doesn't centralize capability. It multiplies it.

That's where reframed leadership begins.

Not as a technique or a personality trait, but as a fundamental shift in orientation—from extracting value to developing it, from directing people to cultivating them, from asking how to get more out of a team to asking what you're putting into them. Everything else in this book builds on that premise.

In the chapters ahead, we'll unpack what this investment actually looks like—how presence shapes trust, how development leads to autonomy, and how all of it compounds over time. But before we go there, we have to lay the foundation, because leadership that isn't rooted in investment will always revert to control, especially under pressure.

So, this is the real starting point.

If someone followed you for years—watched how you handled tension, how you made decisions, how you treated people when things went wrong—what leader would they become?

That question isn't theoretical. People answer it every day.

And once you start paying attention to it, leadership stops being something you do and starts becoming something you leave behind.

Chapter 2 – The ROI of People

If you really want to understand a leader—not the title on their email signature, but the truth of how they operate—don't start with their strategic plan, their mission statements, or the framed values poster in the hallway. Start with their calendar. That's where the real story lives.

A leader's calendar is a quiet confession booth. It reveals what they value, what they avoid, what they prioritize, and—most telling of all—what they are actually funding with their time.

Most leaders say something like, "My people are my greatest asset." It's practically embroidered on half the throw pillows in corporate America. But if their calendars could talk, many would whisper back, "Really? Because we haven't seen you in days."

That disconnect usually isn't rooted in indifference. Most leaders care deeply. But caring isn't the same as investing. And investing isn't the same as being near people—it's choosing, on purpose, to spend limited leadership capital where it multiplies.

There were seasons in my own leadership journey when my calendar betrayed me—weeks filled wall-to-wall with meetings, reports, dashboards, budget cycles, performance metrics, and the constant gravitational pull of operational urgency. Not because I didn't value my people, but because I quietly fell into a trap that catches far more leaders than we like to admit: believing that busyness is the same as productivity, and productivity is the same as leadership.

It's not.

Leadership returns aren't generated by activity alone. They're generated by allocation. Where a leader chooses to place their time determines what actually grows—what gets attention, what gets reinforced, what gets protected, and what gets left to fend for itself.

You can outsource tasks, delegate projects, and automate workflows. But there is one thing a leader cannot outsource: attention. And attention—real, intentional attention—is the rarest currency of leadership in the organization.

So, your calendar is one of your investment strategies.

I once coached an exceptionally sharp leader. Strategic, thoughtful, respected. His mind worked like a well-tuned engine, always processing. Leadership books lined his office shelves, many still pristine. His team admired him, but they didn't feel particularly connected to him. They described him as respectful but distant.

"He's smart, but I don't really know what he thinks of us."

"He's helpful… when we can get time with him."

"I always feel like I'm interrupting."

The heartbreaking part was this: he had no idea.

He wasn't cold or arrogant. He was just relentlessly busy.

When I asked him to walk me through his week, his calendar looked like a Tetris board played by someone with impressive reflexes and terrible boundaries. 14 hours a week were dedicated to preparing and reviewing reports. 14. Valuable data, yes—but data that wasn't changing because the people behind it weren't being invested in.

Then I asked a simple question that stopped him mid-scroll.

"How much of your week is spent developing your people?"

He paused. Scrolled again. Frowned.

"Maybe... an hour," he said.

"Total?" I asked.

"Total."

There it was.

His leadership ROI wasn't low because he lacked care or intention. It was low because his investment strategy was upside down. He was pouring most of his leadership capital into activities that added, while neglecting those that multiplied.

We did not overhaul his role or add anything new. We simply reallocated two of those report hours toward intentional conversations. Nothing flashy. Nothing complicated. Just the presence where it had been missing.

Within a quarter, team performance improved measurably. Not because the work changed. Because the people did.

This is where leadership often gets misunderstood. Investing in people gets labeled a "soft skill," when in reality it's one of the most structurally sound decisions a leader can make. People are not the human side of the business. They are the operating system.

When leaders invest in people, predictable outcomes follow. Not always immediately, and not always cleanly—but reliably over time. Communication improves. Initiative increases. Problems surface earlier, and solutions deepen. Burnout decreases, and performance rises. And overall, culture strengthens.

The returns compound.

And the reverse is equally true.

When leaders withdraw attention—when conversations get delayed, people become interruptions, and leadership slips into managerial autopilot—the returns diminish. Slowly at first. Then unmistakably. Teams don't collapse because of one bad day. They erode from extended periods of leadership absence.

At this point, many leaders, and potentially you, may think, "I don't have time for this. My plate is already full." That's understandable. Every leader is busy. Every role carries more weight than it appears from the outside.

But here is the uncomfortable reality: time is rarely the barrier. Prioritization is.

Leaders make time for what they value. Always.

The leaders who invest in people do not have more hours in the day. They simply refuse to allocate all of their energy to work that doesn't multiply. Tasks add. People multiply. The highest ROI a leader can achieve is in the human beings who advance the mission.

Let's pause here for a minute and take an honest look at your calendar:

Calendar Audit (What You're Actually Funding)

- Pull your last two weeks of calendar data (real, not aspirational).

- Label each block: Adds (operational upkeep) or Multiplies (grows people/capability).

- Circle the top three recurring blocks that consume time but don't change outcomes.

- Create two 30-minute blocks per week labeled "People Investment" (protected like a meeting with your boss).

- Decide on one "default no" category (meetings you won't accept without a clear purpose/agenda).

- Ask: If my calendar is a confession booth, what is it confessing right now?

One of the most surprising discoveries in leadership is how little it takes to make someone feel noticed—and how deeply people crave that experience. Recognition does not require grand gestures. Often, it appears when a leader pauses long enough to ask a sincere question, remember something personal, or acknowledge effort that was not flashy but mattered.

People remember being noticed far longer than they remember being managed.

I once worked with a director whose team was technically competent but emotionally disconnected. She was organized, decisive, and capable—everything her résumé promised. Yet morale lagged. Performance hovered below its potential. When we looked at her calendar, it was immaculate. Color-coded. Optimized. Not a single recurring block dedicated to people.

"I keep meaning to spend more time with them," she said. "But something always comes up."

It always does.

We did not redesign her workflow or change her expectations. We ran a small experiment: 15 minutes each morning, before email, connecting with three people. No agenda, no fixing—just presence.

Two weeks later, the returns arrived—not as metrics, but as narratives. Issues surfaced earlier. Engagement shifted. One employee who had been quietly considering leaving chose to stay. All from a change so small it felt insignificant.

That's the paradox of leadership investment: small moments create outsized returns.

Impact doesn't require intensity. It requires intentionality. And intentionality is usually quiet. It's not dramatic. It doesn't announce itself. But it reshapes how people present themselves over time.

This chapter isn't about how to invest well—we'll unpack that in the chapters ahead. It's about recognizing that investing in people is not a detour from leadership work. It is the work. Presence, trust, development, and autonomy each deserve their own attention, and we'll explore them intentionally as we move forward.

For now, the takeaway is simple and profound.

Most performance problems are, actually, investment problems in disguise. People disengage quietly long before they disengage visibly. You see it in shorter answers, fewer ideas, cautious decisions, and a subtle shift in energy that metrics don't capture until it's too late.

Teams rarely fail from a lack of competence. They fail due to a lack of sustained leadership investment.

And the ROI of people?

It's astonishing—not because people are perfect, but because when leaders invest consistently, people begin to operate differently. They anticipate needs. They take ownership naturally. They solve problems earlier. They multiply excellence beyond what any single leader could produce alone.

Leadership isn't just about building better results. It's about building better people—who, in turn, build better results.

Operating Notes — Put This into Practice

It's easy to agree with leadership principles and still return to the same defaults by Monday morning. These "Do This Next Week" pages are meant to close that gap. They turn the key ideas of each part into a short, practical set of actions, scripts, watch-fors, and questions you can use immediately—without adding more theory.

Actions

- Do a "calendar confession": circle anything that adds activity but doesn't multiply people (status, report prep, endless alignment).

- Move one hour from that bucket into the work that multiplies: a 1:1, a coaching conversation, or a walk-around where you listen more than you talk.

- Pick one leadership pattern you want to change (speed-over-curiosity, solving-too-fast, disappearing into ops) and name it to your team.

- Ask for one piece of truth: "Where do you experience me as helpful—and where do you experience me as heavy?" Then don't defend.

- Choose one moment this week to trade control for investment: let someone else carry the decision, and stay available without hovering.

- At the end of the week, write one sentence: "Because I led this way, my team became _____."

Scripts (use them verbatim if you want)

1. **Reset the posture**

   "I'm taking a hard look at how I lead. I don't just want results—I want people to grow here. What would help you do your best work right now?"

2. **Invite truth without punishment**

   "I want the honest version, not the safe version. If something isn't working, tell me while it's still small. I'll listen before I respond."

Watch-fors

- Mistaking control for competence—especially when pressure hits.

- Measuring leadership only by output, not by who people are becoming.

- Staying "busy" enough to avoid the harder work of presence and investment.

Reflection questions

- If someone followed me for years, what kind of leader would they become?

- Where am I extracting performance instead of investing in people?

- What does my calendar prove—without my words needing to say anything?

Part II: Investing

Most leaders don't lack care—they lack an investment strategy. This part answers a practical question: **what does it look like to invest in people in a way that compounds?** You'll focus on time and attention, trust, and development—not as "soft skills," but as the deposits that build capability over time.

Watch for proximity masquerading as presence, inconsistency that drains trust, and quick fixes that train people to outsource their thinking upward.

Now we move from defining leadership to practicing it.

Chapter 3 – Investing Time and Attention

There's a difference between being available and being present, and most leaders learn that distinction the hard way.

I used to think presence meant proximity. If my door was open, my calendar visible, and my inbox responsive, I assumed I was doing my part. People could reach me. I was accessible. That should count for something, right?

It does. Just not as much as we think.

Availability is logistics. Presence is attention. And attention is not passive. It's directional. It tells people, without words, "what matters here" and "who matters here."

Attention is dignity.

When someone has your full attention—even briefly— they feel it. And when they don't, they feel that too.

Leaders do not need to announce priorities. Attention broadcasts them constantly.

For a long time, I underestimated how powerful that signal really was.

I recall sitting in meetings where I was physically present but mentally elsewhere—half-listening, already forming solutions, already thinking about what came next. I wasn't trying to be dismissive; I was trying to be efficient. But efficiency has a way of flattening people when it replaces curiosity.

Over time, I noticed something subtle happening. People brought conclusions instead of questions. Updates instead of ideas. Safe answers instead of honest ones. Not because they lacked insight, but because they had learned—correctly—that my attention was optimized for speed, not understanding.

That realization landed harder than I expected.

Attention does more than make people feel heard. It creates meaning. When a leader slows down enough to stay with someone's thought—to follow it, not rush it—it communicates that thinking matters here, not just execution. That message shapes behavior far more effectively than any slogan ever could.

And it's why time and attention aren't soft skills. It's a leadership decision.

Presence is a signal.

I learned that in an unexpected place—on a morning that had nothing to do with leadership theory and everything to do with being human.

We had just opened a new primary care practice. The kind of opening that feels like controlled chaos—construction dust still settling, workflows half-built, phones ringing before you're fully staffed. My days were full and fast. Every minute felt claimed. I was moving in ten directions at once, trying to keep the wheels from coming off.

That morning, a police officer approached the front desk and requested to speak with me.

When I came out, he kept his voice low, professional. He said an elderly man had been living in his car in our parking lot. He asked if I wanted him removed.

I nodded like I understood the question, but my mind immediately went to what leaders default to under pressure—liability, policy, precedent. I followed him outside, expecting a quick logistical conversation about property lines and protocol.

Instead, I saw a man whose exhaustion was heavier than anything in his backseat.

The car wasn't a "situation." It was a shelter. The windows had that faint haze from sleeping. The seat was reclined the way it gets when a body tries to disappear. He looked up at me like he already knew how this ends—another door closed, another "not here."

In that moment, something in me slowed down.

Not because I had a plan. Not because I'm unusually compassionate. Because I made a choice leaders rarely make when the calendar is full: I chose to stay.

I walked over. I introduced myself. I asked his name.

He answered carefully, like names can be used against you when you've been on the wrong side of enough conversations. He explained—without drama, without self-pity—that life had unraveled. The story wasn't neat. It wasn't polished. It was just a human being trying to survive.

I don't remember making a calculated decision. I recall giving him my attention long enough to see him as more than a problem to be removed.

So, I told the officer he could stay—for now.

That was it—no grand gestures, no committee, no policy memo.

Just a few minutes of invested attention.

Those minutes changed the subsequent few months.

Because what happened next wasn't orchestrated leadership. It was what time and attention make possible inside a healthy culture: other people noticed what I noticed, and they moved toward it.

My team did what teams do when they feel ownership—and when they believe attention is allowed.

They brought him groceries. Quietly. Consistently. Not as charity, but as care. Someone arrived with household goods and left them without turning it into an interaction. Another brought clothes. They learned his name, said it as it mattered, and treated him like he belonged to the category "human," not the category "problem."

They made him part of the family.

He showered in our bathroom.

That sentence still stops me—not because it's dramatic, but because it's so practical. Real attention doesn't just feel warm; it does something. It restores dignity in ways that don't photograph well or fit into a KPI.

Over the next few weeks, he came inside more. At first, it was for water. Then it was for conversation. Then it was simply because people wanted him to be seen—seen without being fixed, seen without being managed.

Eventually, he became a patient of ours. In that process, they discovered that he was due retroactive financial benefits he had never received. Not a small amount—enough to change his trajectory if he could access it.

My team didn't just feel bad about that.

They stayed with it.

They helped him navigate forms, phone calls, and follow-ups—the kind of slow, frustrating work that breaks people who are already exhausted. They did what invested attention always does: they kept showing up after the first "good deed" glow wears off. They didn't drop it when it got inconvenient.

When the money finally came through, it wasn't a miracle. It was the compound return of consistent attention.

And that money became the key.

An apartment down the street.

A job.

A life that stabilized—not overnight, but for real.

Here's the leadership takeaway, and it sits right in the heart of this chapter:

I wasn't the hero of this story. I was the first signal.

My "move" was small: I paused long enough to pay attention. But in a culture, the leader's attention is a spotlight. Whatever you slow down for becomes important. Whatever you rush past becomes optional.

By staying with him for a few minutes, I told my team—without saying a word—that people matter here. That dignity lies in not outsourcing humanity.

And they took it from there.

That's what time and attention do when they're invested well. They don't just make someone feel seen. They create a standard that spreads.

If my team had needed permission for every step, none of it would have happened. If they were afraid of being second-guessed, they would have stayed in their lane. If we had a culture of "not my job," he would have been escorted off the property and out of our story.

But they didn't wait.

Because invested time and attention don't just help the person in front of you—they also train everyone watching what ownership looks like.

Attention is a form of dignity. And consistent attention is how dignity becomes culture.

That's the compounding return.

That lesson didn't appear on the dashboard. But it changed the atmosphere of that place in ways no process improvement ever could.

This is where leaders often misunderstand the concept of attention. They assume it has to be dramatic to matter. It doesn't. Most of the time, attention is quiet. It appears in pauses, not in pronouncements. In staying a few seconds longer instead of rushing on. In choosing to notice what would be easier to overlook.

There's also a common fear hiding underneath leadership busyness—the fear that attention will turn into micromanagement. That if we get too close, we'll get in the way. However, attention and control are not the same. One is about understanding. The other is about interference.

Micromanagement constrains people. Attention anchors them.

Leaders who invest attention early often find they're needed less later—not because they withdrew, but because people steadied under that investment. Attention shortens the distance between what's happening and what gets named. It allows leaders to hear about things while they're still small, still workable, still human-sized.

There's an emotional consequence of a leader's availability that rarely gets discussed. When leaders consistently make time—unhurried time—people stop rehearsing their conversations. They stop filtering as much. They stop waiting for the "right moment" that never seems to come. The relationship relaxes. When relationships relax, information flows more freely.

This doesn't require long meetings or elaborate structures. Some of the most impactful leadership moments are surprisingly brief. A focused five-minute conversation can carry more weight than an hour spent half-distracted. What matters isn't duration. It's quality.

I've watched leaders transform teams not by adding more meetings, but by changing how they show up in the ones they already have. Phones down, eyes up—unrushed questions, and silence you don't rush to fill. Those small shifts send a powerful signal: "You're worth my time."

And people respond to that signal.

Attention also clarifies identity. When leaders consistently recognize effort, thinking, and growth—not just outcomes—people learn what matters in contribution. Over time, behavior follows attention. People move toward what gets noticed.

Of course, investing attention isn't always comfortable. It slows you down. It exposes you to uncertainty, emotion, and complexity. Sometimes you'll leave a conversation without a solution, unsure whether you helped at all.

But presence itself is help.

People aren't looking for leaders with perfect answers. They're looking for leaders willing to stay with the question long enough to understand it. That willingness builds something beneath the surface—something we'll explore more fully in the chapters ahead.

For now, what matters is this: attention is not a soft gesture. It's a leadership investment with real consequences. Where attention goes, confidence follows. Where attention is absent, uncertainty fills the gap.

Presence Protocol (Try This Week)

- In your next three conversations, do one thing: don't multitask (phone down, eyes up).

- Ask one slow question before you solve: "What are you most unsure about right now?"

- Repeat back one sentence: "What I hear you saying is…" (then stop).

- Leave two beats of silence before responding— long enough for the real thought to appear.

- End with one ownership line: "What do you think the next right step is?"

- Afterward, rate yourself: did they leave feeling processed—or seen?

So, here's the question worth sitting with before we move forward:

When people leave a conversation with you, do they feel processed—or do they feel seen?

That answer will tell you more about your leadership than any calendar ever could.

Chapter 4 – Investing Trust

You can feel trust before anyone explains it. Walk into a room where it's strong, and everything moves with less friction—questions come early, disagreements don't spike the temperature, and decisions don't require a second meeting just to confirm what everyone already understood. Nothing about it is flashy. That's what makes it easy to underestimate.

But when trust is thin, you feel that too. Conversations get careful. People edit themselves in real time. The truth arrives late, if it arrives at all. And the leader starts working twice as hard to get half the traction—paying for the gap with energy, attention, and time.

Trust is the quietest force in leadership, and the most expensive to lose.

You rarely notice it when it's strong. Teams just move. Conversations happen without drama. People bring you problems early, not when they've already become emergencies. Decisions don't feel like hostage negotiations. You don't need a second meeting to clarify what was meant in the first. It's not flashy, but it's steady—and steadiness is underrated until you have lived without it.

But when trust is thin, you feel it immediately. The room gets cautious. Questions come wrapped in disclaimers. People "circle back" privately before they say anything publicly. Creativity gets replaced with safe execution. And you start working twice as hard to get half the traction, which is a cruel arrangement, especially when you're the one paying for it with your energy.

Trust is the one leadership investment with no shortcuts.

You can't demand it or buy it. You can't bluff your way into it with a motivational speech and a catered lunch.

Trust doesn't care about your slide deck. Trust cares about your patterns.

If leadership had a stock exchange, trust would be your blue-chip asset—boring at first glance, not nearly as exciting as charisma or big vision statements, but astonishing in long-term returns. It compounds quietly. It stabilizes everything else. It turns influence into something durable. And it's also the only asset I know that can be wiped out by one careless moment, like spilling coffee on a laptop you swear you backed up.

That's the part no one tells you: trust is either your greatest leadership advantage or your greatest leadership tax. Without it, everything costs more. Every decision requires extra explanation, and every change requires extra reassurance. Every tough conversation requires an emotional down payment to get in the door.

And unlike skill, knowledge, or charisma, trust cannot be faked. People always know. You can fake enthusiasm and confidence. You can even fake knowing what "synergy" means in the wild. But trust? Trust exposes you.

The simplest way I've found to understand trust is this: every person you lead has an account for you. Every interaction is either a deposit or a withdrawal.

- A kept promise? Deposit.

- Following up when you said you would? Deposit.

- Owning a mistake without defensiveness? Deposit.

- Changing your mind and explaining why? Deposit.

- A broken commitment? Withdrawal.

- A "we'll see" that never becomes anything? Withdrawal.

- A tone that doesn't match your words? Withdrawal.

- A leader who says, "My door is always open," but looks like a dragon guarding a cave of gold? Major withdrawal.

That's the math of trust: it grows by teaspoons and drains by gallons. I know that ratio isn't fair, but leadership never has been. Leadership is just real.

Most leaders assume you build trust in dramatic moments—crisis meetings, bold decisions, heroic saves. Sometimes it is. But more often, you build trust in the quiet—through patterns, not proclamations. People don't believe what you announce. They believe what you repeat. That's why trust is so connected to a word that sounds unexciting but is wildly powerful: consistency.

Consistency isn't perfection. It's reliability. It's the same leader on Tuesday afternoon that you were on Monday morning. It's people knowing what version of you they're going to get. It's the gift of predictability in a world where everything else feels uncertain.

And predictability isn't boring to your team. Predictability is restful.

When people can predict you, their nervous system relaxes. They stop doing emotional math. They no longer carry umbrellas everywhere "just in case." They stop bracing for weather changes in your tone, your reactions, your moods. They stop wondering whether today is a good day to ask a question or a terrible day to exist near your calendar.

You can be tough, direct, quirky, highly structured—people can handle a lot of leadership styles. What they cannot handle is inconsistency. Inconsistency forces everyone into constant interpretation: "Are you approachable today or brittle? Curious or hurried? Collaborative or controlling? Open to feedback or quietly offended by it?"

When people can't predict your emotional weather, they start protecting themselves. And self-protection is the enemy of trust.

I've seen this play out in leaders who aren't cruel, aren't arrogant, and aren't even aware they're doing damage. They're just stressed. They're carrying too much. Their tone sharpens under pressure. Their patience thins. Their words speed up. Their face does something their heart never authorized.

What's happening to the leader is understandable—and what's happening in the team is predictable. Because people don't experience your intentions, they experience your impact.

This is what I call Accidental Volatility: a leader whose demeanor shifts so dramatically when stressed that the team begins managing the leader's mood rather than focusing on the work. No one will say it out loud, because people don't like admitting they are afraid of a leader who "isn't scary." But you'll see it in other ways: filtered feedback, delayed bad news, cautious decisions, a room that tightens instead of loosens.

Trust doesn't require you to be calm at all times. It requires you to be anchored—someone your team can predict under pressure. They need to believe you won't swing from supportive to suspicious, from curious to accusatory, from collaborative to cold the moment things get tense. A team can handle pressure. What it can't handle is pressure plus unpredictability from the person holding the authority.

So, **consistency** is one pillar of trust. But trust has a second pillar: **transparency**.

People don't need you to have all the answers. They just need you to tell the truth. When leaders hide information, speak in riddles, or avoid difficult conversations, people don't stay neutral. They fill the gaps with assumptions, and those assumptions are rarely positive.

I have observed trust collapse within a team, not because the leader was unkind or incompetent, but because he communicated in a fog. Every update felt like a coded message. Every decision came with a half-explanation wrapped in corporate air freshener. The team started whispering theories. Fear moved into the space where reality should have been. And by the time the truth surfaced, the issue wasn't even the decision—it was the secrecy.

Transparency isn't oversharing. It's alignment. It's naming reality clearly enough that people don't have to guess. It's saying, "Here's what we know. Here's what we don't. Here's what we're doing next." That honesty does something profound: it treats people like adults. And adults can handle hard news. Adults struggle most when leaders manage by omission.

Trust is built through **reliability**, too. This is the third pillar of trust. It's the simple act of doing what you said you'd do. This sounds obvious, and that's why it's so dangerous. Leaders assume it's covered. Leaders assume the "big stuff" matters and the "small stuff" doesn't. But trust doesn't separate your commitments into categories. A follow-up is a follow-up. A promise is a promise. And nothing makes a leader feel less trustworthy than being consistently "almost" reliable.

Here's a pattern I've seen more times than I can count: leaders overpromise because they want to be helpful. They say yes quickly. They offer reassurance. They hand out commitments like they're free samples at Costco. Then reality hits—meetings, crises, urgent fires—and the follow-through gets delayed, forgotten, or quietly dropped. Most of the time, the leader doesn't even realize what they've done. But the team does.

When someone has to follow up on what you said you'd deliver, it breeds frustration. It subtly reclassifies their view: "This leader's words are optional."

And once your words become optional, your influence becomes expensive.

This is why trust isn't built through speeches. It's built through what you do when no one is grading you, no one is watching, and no one is rewarding you for being consistent. Trust is the accumulated evidence that you are who you say you are.

Now, at this point, some leaders feel discouraged because they think, "So you're telling me if I ever drop a ball, it's over?"

No. (trust me, I've dropped more balls than I can count)

Trust doesn't require perfection. It requires repair. Every leader breaks trust at some point—not because they're malicious, but because they're human. A missed follow-up. A poorly timed comment. A promise made too quickly. A stressful day where your tone outruns your intentions. A moment where exhaustion wins.

Trust is fragile, not because people are overly sensitive, but because leadership carries weight. Your words echo. Your actions ripple. Your inconsistencies don't stay small. But repair is what separates leaders who grow influence from leaders who slowly lose it. Repair is the skill no one ever taught most leaders, and it's one of the most powerful trust investments you can make because it signals something deeper than competence: it signals humility.

When trust breaks—even slightly—most leaders are tempted to do one of three things: ignore it, justify it, or outrun it with productivity. None of those restores trust. They just delay the consequences.

Repair starts with a different courage: the courage to circle back.

There are three actions I've seen and have tried that consistently rebuild trust when something goes wrong.

First, name what happened—clearly, calmly, and without excuses. People don't need a dissertation on your intentions. They don't need qualifiers wrapped around accountability like bubble wrap. They need you to say, "I missed that," or "I handled that poorly," or "I should have followed up sooner." When leaders skip this step—when they pretend nothing happened—people carry the weight alone, and silence becomes its own statement.

Second, acknowledge impact, not just intention. Intentions matter, but impact shapes the relationship. When leaders focus only on intent, people feel unseen; when they own their impact, people feel respected. It sounds like: "I can see how that created confusion," or "I recognize that my tone shut down the conversation," or "I understand that my delay put you in a difficult spot." Notice what's missing: defensiveness. Defensiveness is the enemy of repair because it says, "I want to be understood more than I want to understand you."

Third, demonstrate change through renewed consistency. Nothing rebuilds trust faster than consistently aligned behavior. Not one grand gesture. Not a dramatic apology tour. Just visible progress. People do not need instant transformation. They need evidence. They need to experience the change long enough for their nervous system to recognize it as real.

Trust repair is less like flipping a switch and more like strengthening a muscle. Consistency does the heavy lifting.

Now, there's one final trust builder that is often misunderstood: **vulnerability**. This is pillar number four.

Not oversharing. Not emotional theatrics. Not "confessional leadership," where your team becomes your therapist, and you call it "authenticity." I'm talking about the vulnerability that says, "I'm human too," without dumping your weight onto everyone else.

It sounds like: "I don't have the answer yet." "That decision didn't land the way I hoped." "I missed something, and I'm correcting it." "I need your perspective."

People do not trust leaders who pretend to have no cracks. They trust leaders who navigate their cracks with honesty.

Vulnerability does not weaken authority; it strengthens credibility. It turns leadership from a protected performance into a shared reality. And when people feel like they are dealing with a person—not a persona—trust becomes more reciprocal. People share concerns sooner. They surface issues earlier. They tell the truth about what is not working. They offer ideas without first having to armor them.

That is the real test of trust on a team: are people willing to bring you the truth?

Truth is what's working and what's not, their mistakes and yours, and the realities that never show up on dashboards. When people trust their leader, truth flows; when they fear their leader, truth hides. And truth is the currency of healthy teams—trust is what puts that currency into circulation.

This is why trust and performance are not separate. A team with strong trust can move quickly because they are not spending energy covering their backs. They are not busy building emotional armor or rehearsing every sentence. They are not waiting for a meeting after the meeting where the real decisions are made.

They simply act

And when trust is thin, everything becomes heavier. Conversations drag, decisions slow, and innovation narrows as confirmation multiplies. You can still move, but it feels like towing a trailer with the parking brake on.

Trust is the difference between effort and momentum.

So, if Chapter 3 was about the dignity of attention, this chapter is about what happens when attention becomes reliability—when leaders become steady enough, honest enough, and humble enough that people stop wondering whether they can rely on them.

In the next chapter, we'll move into development—how leaders multiply capability without turning every conversation into correction. And later, we'll explore how trust becomes the foundation for psychological safety, because safety doesn't appear out of nowhere; it grows in the soil of trust.

Trust warrants its own examination first, because without it, every other leadership practice incurs greater costs than it should.

Before we move on, sit with this:

If your team had to describe you with one word, would it be "consistent"?

If not, what would have to change—not in your intentions, but in your patterns—for trust to start compounding again?

Chapter 5 – Investing in Development

Most leaders want their people to grow. That part is easy to say. The harder part is resisting the instinct to jump in and fix things when growth looks messy.

Early in my leadership journey, I confused development with correction. When something went wrong, I stepped in quickly—sometimes too quickly—because I felt responsible. I thought I was helping. In reality, I was often short-circuiting learning.

Correction is efficient. Development is not.

Correction produces immediate improvement.
Development produces long-term capability.

And if you're not careful, the pressure for short-term results will quietly train you to choose speed over growth every time.

That's the tension at the heart of leadership development.

Correcting fixes today's answer; developing builds someone who gets it right again—and better—next time.

Those are different goals.

Coaching lives on the development side of that line. Coaching doesn't ignore mistakes, but it treats them as raw material rather than failures. A coaching posture says, "Let's understand how you're thinking," instead of, "Here's what you should've done." It slows the moment just enough for learning to take place.

That pause matters more than most leaders realize.

When leaders default to correcting, people begin outsourcing their thinking upward. They wait, defer, and play it safe. Not because they lack ability, but because they've learned that initiative will be overwritten anyway. Over time, the leader becomes the smartest person in the room—while everyone else quietly stops stretching.

Development requires a different investment.

It asks leaders to tolerate imperfection in the service of growth. It asks for patience when a faster solution is available. It asks leaders to believe that the long game is worth playing, even when the short game is loud and demanding.

Before we talk about how leaders develop people well, we need to acknowledge something harder.

Development is not clean. Development doesn't move in straight lines—and it doesn't come with guarantees. When you take responsibility for growing others, you also take responsibility for the complexity they carry with them— much of which will never show up on a résumé, a KPI dashboard, or a performance review.

Many leadership books tell success stories.

This one has to make room for the kind of story that leaves a mark.

The lesson that changed me most didn't come from something I did brilliantly. It came from a situation I mishandled—one that still carries weight decades later.

Early in my leadership journey, I hired a man—let's call him Sam—who, at first, looked like exactly the kind of person you want on your team. Steady. Capable. Committed. He worked hard. He showed up. He had that quiet reliability that makes you breathe a sigh of relief as a leader.

And then, slowly, the edges started to fray.

It wasn't one dramatic collapse. It was the small things that didn't fit together at first. A late arrival. A missed shift. A moment where his eyes looked like they hadn't slept in days. He started showing up disheveled. His focus scattered. His energy felt unsettled—like he was present in body but somewhere else in spirit—the kind of "somewhere else" you can't put into a write-up.

I noticed. Of course, I noticed.

But I didn't know what I was seeing.

Then, a belligerent patient incident happened in the clinic, and the next day, Sam brought a gun to work "for protection."

That moment is seared into me.

Not because it was dramatic—because it was clarifying. My gut didn't whisper. It shouted. Something was terribly wrong.

And here's where I wish I could rewrite the page.

I did what I knew how to do at the time: I tried to manage it like a performance issue. I documented. I corrected. I had conversations. I toggled between stern and soft, between discipline and compassion, as if I had found the perfect tone that would unlock the situation.

But nothing really changed.

Because the truth is, Sam wasn't battling a "work problem." He was battling something deeper. And I kept trying to lead him out of a place that required more than leadership.

Fear and uncertainty clouded my decisions. I didn't want to overreact and crush someone who might just be having a hard season. I also didn't want to underreact and ignore a situation that could hurt someone. So, I hovered in the worst possible middle—always responding, never truly intervening. Always talking, never truly seeing.

Eventually, believing I had exhausted my options, I let him go.

Shortly thereafter, I learned that the police arrested him for burglary and drug-related charges. He spent the next six months in jail.

And then—completely unexpectedly—we ran into each other.

It was the same day they released him.

I can still picture it: the surprise of seeing him there, the strange collision of two timelines—my life moving forward, his life trying to restart. He looked at me with tears in his eyes, shook my hand (and didn't let go), and thanked me. Not for firing him. Not for the warnings. For the fact that I had hired him in the first place. He told me that for a while, that job made him believe he could be something different. That someone saw something in him when other people didn't.

Then he said he wanted to turn his life around.

And he asked if I'd be willing to be part of that process.

I said yes.

Of course I did.

Part relief, part hope, part that deep human instinct that says, "Maybe this is the moment where it turns."

I was excited. Maybe a do-over for him *and* for me.

That night, he took his own life...

What I needed to hear back then—and what I want to name clearly now—is this: a leader is not a clinician, and leadership presence is not a substitute for professional care. Your role is not to diagnose, counsel, or carry a mental health crisis alone.

Your role is to **notice**, **respond with humanity**, and **escalate appropriately**. If someone mentions suicide, self-harm, or you have any reason to believe they may be a danger to themselves, treat it as urgent.

In a workplace, that means involving the right support immediately—HR, your organization's employee assistance resources, and emergency services when needed. Don't worry about "overreacting." In moments like this, caution is not drama. It's a responsibility. You can be compassionate and still be clear about boundaries: stay present, stay calm, and connect with people trained to help.

For decades, that moment has carved a quiet ache into my leadership. I replayed every decision. Every conversation. Every hesitation. I wondered what might have changed if I'd slowed down sooner—if I'd asked different questions, if I'd looked past the behavior to the pain underneath it, if I'd had the courage to name what I didn't know and pull in more help instead of trying to handle it alone.

I can't undo the past. But I can refuse to waste it.

That experience taught me something no framework ever could: development is not a formula, and leadership is not risk-free.

Leadership will hand you moments you wish you could redo—moments you would pay dearly to rewrite. Some lessons don't offer closure. They offer responsibility. They remind you that leadership isn't about perfection. It's stewardship—of people, of standards, of safety, of dignity.

And sometimes stewardship means slowing down early enough to see what's really happening.

Because when you miss that moment—when you keep treating pain like performance—the cost can follow you a lot longer than the lesson itself.

Stories like this resist tidy conclusions, and they should. Not every leadership moment resolves into clarity or closure. Some remain unfinished, pressing quietly on your conscience long after the season has passed. But if leadership is truly about development, then even the moments that haunt us must be allowed to teach us— shaping how carefully we listen, how thoughtfully we intervene, and how seriously we carry the responsibility of investing in another human life.

One of the most effective ways leaders cultivate development is through stretch—not pressure, but stretch. Stretch assignments place individuals just beyond their current comfort zone, where effort is required, and learning is unavoidable. The key is intention. Stretch without support feels like abandonment; stretch with context becomes opportunity.

Good leaders pay attention to who is ready for stretch, when it's appropriate, and what area of growth it's meant to unlock. They don't hand out challenges randomly. They curate them thoughtfully, aligning opportunity with potential.

And this is where delegation takes on an entirely different meaning.

Most leaders view delegation as a way to reduce workload. Get tasks off your plate. Free up time. Increase efficiency. All of that matters—but development-minded leaders see delegation as a design tool. They ask not only, "What needs to be done?" but also, "Who could grow by doing this?"

Delegation becomes developmental when it transfers thinking, not just tasks.

Handing someone a checklist is helpful. Handing them responsibility for outcomes is formative. The difference is subtle, but powerful. One builds capacity. The other builds dependence.

Leaders who invest in development are intentional about what they retain and what they relinquish—not because they want less responsibility, but because they want others to grow into more.

That leadership requires systems, not just good intentions.

Development doesn't scale through occasional conversations or isolated mentoring moments. It scales through structures that make growth predictable. Clear growth pathways. Regular feedback rhythms. Opportunities to reflect, practice, and progress. These systems need not be complex, but they must be consistent.

Without systems, development depends entirely on the leader's bandwidth. With systems in place, development becomes part of the culture.

Future leaders aren't developed by accident. They're developed because someone thought ahead—created space for learning, allowed room for failure, and resisted the urge to rescue too quickly. They're shaped through repeated exposure to responsibility, reflection, and refinement.

This is where many leaders get discouraged. Development feels slow. Progress isn't always linear. Sometimes the person you're investing in struggles more before they succeed. That's normal. Growth often appears as regression before it appears as mastery.

The leaders who remain committed through that phase are the ones who multiply capability rather than hoard it.

Growth pathways matter here. People need a sense of trajectory—not just promotions, but progression. They need to know that effort leads somewhere, that learning compounds, that today's stretch connects to tomorrow's opportunity. When leaders help people see that arc, motivation deepens. Development stops feeling like extra work and starts feeling like forward motion.

This doesn't require a perfectly mapped career ladder. It requires conversation, clarity of intent, and follow-through. People don't need guarantees. They need direction and belief.

Development also changes how leaders measure success. Instead of asking, "Did this get done well?" they begin asking, "Did this make someone stronger?" Over time, that shift transforms teams. Capability spreads. Initiative increases. Leadership stops bottlenecking at the top.

And here's the quiet truth beneath all of it: leaders who invest in development don't become less necessary. They become more impactful.

Their influence multiplies because it resides in others.

This is where development naturally points forward.

When capability grows, independence follows. Not immediately. Not automatically. But inevitably. That next transition—where development becomes independence—is what we'll explore in Part III. Empowerment is not the starting point of growth; it's the outcome of sustained development.

For now, the work is both simpler and harder.

Are you correcting people so work improves, or are you developing people so capacity expands?

The answer to that question determines whether your leadership scales—or stalls.

Operating Notes — Put This into Practice

This week, trade correction for development—make one deliberate investment that expands someone's capacity instead of reinforcing dependence.

Actions

- Run another highlight every hour you spent on dashboards/reports/ops vs. people. Don't judge it—just see it.

- Reallocate two hours: pull one "adds" block (status/report prep) and move it into two 30-minute development conversations.

- Practice presence on purpose: in your next three meetings, phone down, eyes up, and ask one slow question before you solve anything.

- Make five trust deposits: keep a promise, follow up when you said you would, own a miss without defensiveness, explain a changed decision, match tone to words.

- Close the loop on commitments: write down the open "I'll get back to you" items and either deliver or renegotiate with a new date.

- Coach once instead of correcting: when someone brings a problem, resist the quick fix and stay with their thinking for two minutes.

Scripts (use them verbatim if you want)

1. **Repair / "circle back"**

   "I missed that. That's on me. I can see how it affected you/us. Here's what I'm changing starting now."

2. **Coaching posture**

   "Walk me through how you're thinking. What options have you considered? What feels like your next best step?"

Watch-fors

- Accidental volatility: your tone sharpens under pressure and the team starts managing your mood.

- Overpromising: handing out commitments like free samples, then going quiet when the week gets loud.

- Correction addiction: fixing fast and accidentally training people to outsource their thinking upward.

Reflection questions

- What does my calendar confess about what I truly fund with time?

- Where have I made withdrawals lately—and where is a repair conversation overdue?

- Who on my team is shrinking because I'm optimizing for speed instead of growth?

Part III: Empowering

Empowerment is the handoff that enables autonomy. This part answers the question: **how do you transfer ownership without creating chaos?** You'll build clarity, psychological safety, and communication that invites judgment—not just compliance.

Watch for "empowerment" that is really delegation, safety confused with comfort, and asking for input while punishing honesty.

Here, leadership stops being something you hold and becomes something you share.

Chapter 6 – The Anatomy of Empowerment

If investing in people is the engine of leadership, empowerment is the moment you finally let that engine leave the garage.

Up to now, everything we've discussed remains within a leader's control. You can invest in people, build trust, develop capability—and still quietly keep the wheel in your hands. The work moves. Progress happens. Results show up. And yet, something remains strangely dependent—decisions bottleneck. Initiative hesitates. People wait just a beat longer than they should.

That beat is the sound of unclaimed ownership.

Empowerment is where leadership stops being impressive and starts being scalable (the ability to grow output or revenue without a matching increase in cost, headcount, or complexity). It's where potential turns into motion. And it's also where many leaders discover just how attached they are to being needed.

Most leaders genuinely believe they empower their people. They use the language. They encourage ideas. They affirm effort. They say things like, "Run with it," and "I trust you," and "You've got this." On the surface, it sounds right. But when you watch closely, another pattern often emerges. Decisions still require approval. Solutions still get quietly rewritten. Authority is delegated, only to be recalled when uncertainty arises.

That is not leadership, it's LEASH-ERSHIP... It's empowerment with a leash. And it fails every time.

I've seen leaders cheer for ownership while hovering just close enough to reclaim it the moment discomfort rises. Not out of malice. Out of anxiety. Control feels safe—and it can feel responsible. Control feels like leadership—especially when the stakes are high.

But control, no matter how polished, always limits growth.

Empowerment asks something far more uncomfortable. It asks leaders to give people real responsibility and then resist the urge to rescue them from the weight of it. That's the line most leaders struggle to cross. Not because they don't want others to succeed, but because letting go forces a reckoning with identity.

If I'm not the one steering, what is my role now?

This is where delegation and empowerment often get confused. Delegation moves tasks. Empowerment moves ownership. One transfers work—the other transfers thinking. And the difference is not semantic—it's structural.

When leaders delegate, they often retain decision rights while transferring execution. The work is completed, but its form never changes. When leaders empower, they hand over outcomes. They invite people to design the path rather than merely follow it. That's when creativity enters the room. That's when people stop performing at a high level and start building it.

Ownership changes posture—people sit, speak, and decide differently. They stop asking, "Is this what you want?" and start asking, "Is this better?" That shift is subtle, but once it happens, it's impossible to unsee.

Empowerment, however, is not abandonment. And this is where leaders sometimes swing too far in the other direction.

Empowerment = responsibility + authority + support

Removing any one of these results in frustration, exposure, or dependence.

Real empowerment holds all three together. Responsibility gives the work weight. Authority gives it legitimacy. Support provides the safety for growth. Remove any one of those, and empowerment collapses into something else entirely—confusion, fear, or theater.

This is why empowerment feels risky. It is risky. It redistributes risk from the leader to the system. And leaders who don't acknowledge that risk tend to undermine empowerment the moment something goes sideways. They step back in "just this once." They tighten oversight "temporarily." They retain decision-making authority "until things stabilize."

But people notice.

Empowerment doesn't fail loudly. It erodes quietly—one reclaimed decision at a time.

Most leaders assume the biggest barrier to empowerment is employee readiness. In reality, the bigger barrier is leader anxiety. When leaders feel uncertain, overwhelmed, or exposed, control becomes a reflex. We add layers. We request reasonable updates, but they are accumulating into surveillance. We reframe intervention as quality control.

Sometimes it is. Often, it's the fear of wearing a professional outfit.

Empowerment requires leaders to stay present without steering. To remain accountable for the environment without being the answer to every question. To allow people to experience the stretch of responsibility long enough for confidence to catch up with capability.

That stretch is uncomfortable for everyone.

People rarely step into ownership perfectly. They hesitate. They second-guess. They try things that almost work. Leaders who equate imperfection with incompetence will withdraw empowerment too soon. Leaders who tolerate the learning curve create room for growth that no amount of instruction ever could.

I've seen what that tolerance can unlock.

A few years ago, I took on the work of turning around a market that had been stuck in the bottom five of company performance for so long it felt permanent. The culture was tense. Patients were frustrated. Staff were exhausted. The numbers told the same story the hallways did—nothing was working, and no one believed it would.

In the middle of that strain was a leader who didn't stand out on paper. She wasn't seasoned or polished. If you judged her by credentials alone, you might have assumed she was holding the role until someone more qualified arrived.

However, she had something more difficult to teach.

Hunger.

Not ambition. Hunger. A restless, unrefined drive to prove—to herself most of all—that she was capable of more than her circumstances suggested. It wasn't graceful or contained. It was raw potential, the kind that can either reshape a culture or destabilize it.

So instead of stepping in front of her, I walked alongside her.

Literally.

We logged miles together. Through workflows. Down hallways. Into early-morning data reviews and late conversations that revealed more in the pauses than the answers. Development started with proximity—not oversight, not correction, but shared visibility.

We didn't begin by fixing her. We began by understanding how she thought, what she feared, and where she reacted and hesitated. Where she had strength she didn't yet trust.

Then we widened the lens. We studied the system together—the fractures in communication, the ambiguity in expectations, the patterns underneath the metrics. Not to overwhelm her, but to orient her.

Piece by piece, we built something that looked less like a checklist and more like an apprenticeship.

We practiced setting expectations instead of hoping for them.

We worked through hard conversations before they happened.

We translated numbers into decisions instead of judgments.

When she became overwhelmed—and she did—I didn't take the wheel. But I didn't disappear either.

We made one decision at a time. One conversation at a time. One step forward without rushing the next.

And slowly, something shifted. Not externally at first. Internally.

Her posture changed. Her questions sharpened. Her reactions softened—not because she disengaged, but because she understood. Her team leaned in. Decisions settled. Confidence followed competence instead of trying to outrun it.

After a year, her market had become the leading one in the region.
At 18 months, she was among the top performers in the company.

The same leaders who once questioned whether she belonged became the leaders who believed she could solve any challenge placed before her team.

That's what empowerment uncovers.

It doesn't create brilliance. It creates conditions in which brilliance no longer requires permission.

Over time, empowerment matures in stages. Not formally. Not on a chart. But experientially. Initially, people seek direction. Then they start offering ideas. Eventually, they act with increasing confidence and reflect on outcomes rather than waiting for evaluation—the leader's role shifts alongside that growth—from directing to calibrating to witnessing.

This is where empowerment truly shows its value. It doesn't create brilliance. It uncovers it.

Most teams already have insight sitting quietly in the room. Ideas that haven't been voiced. Solutions that haven't been trusted. Perspectives you haven't invited into the work. Empowerment creates space for those things to surface— not because people suddenly became smarter, but because the environment finally allowed them to contribute fully.

When leaders stop positioning themselves as the center of every decision, teams begin solving problems closer to where they actually live. Momentum increases. Bottlenecks loosen. The organization becomes faster, not slower, because leadership and decision-making are no longer concentrated at the top.

And something shifts inside the leader as well.

Empowerment forces a redefinition of success. Instead of measuring leadership by how indispensable you are, you begin measuring it by how capable others become. That transition can feel like a loss at first, especially for leaders who built their identity around being the fixer, the closer, the one who steps in when things get hard.

But it isn't a loss.

It's graduation.

The leaders who embrace empowerment discover something unexpected: they don't become irrelevant. They become more influential. Their leadership endures in decisions they didn't make, solutions they didn't design, and outcomes they didn't personally influence. Influence expands when it no longer requires permission.

This is the hinge point of Leadership Reframed for a reason. Everything before empowerment prepares for this moment. Investment, trust, development—all of it leads here. Everything that follows depends on how well this transition is managed.

Because empowerment is not the end of leadership involvement, it's the beginning of leadership distribution.

In the chapters ahead, we'll explore what happens when empowerment becomes cultural—when people contribute leadership without waiting to be asked, and when trust creates the conditions for honest dialogue and learning. But empowerment has to come first. Without it, leadership stays centralized. With it, leadership multiplies.

So before we move on, sit with this:

Where are you seeking ownership while still retaining authority?

Where are you offering authority without enough support?

And where are you ready—truly ready—to hand someone the keys and step back far enough for them to realize what they're capable of?

Empowerment is the moment leadership begins to move without your pushing it.

And that's when you know you've built something that lasts.

Chapter 7 – Creating Psychological Safety

If empowerment is the spark that ignites people, psychological safety is the oxygen that sustains the flame.

You can hand someone real responsibility. You can give them authority that actually means something. You can say all the right things about trust, ownership, and initiative. But if people don't feel safe enough to admit they're unsure, confused, or overwhelmed, empowerment becomes a framed idea that never leaves the wall— impressive to look at, impossible to breathe.

This is the part leaders often underestimate.

Empowerment doesn't fail because people lack talent. It fails because people don't trust what will happen to them when they take a risk, and the outcome isn't guaranteed. Psychological safety enables empowered action to persist over time—not because it makes work easier, but because it makes honesty survivable.

Fear in organizations is rarely dramatic. It doesn't stomp into meetings wearing combat boots. More often, it slips in quietly and takes a seat. It shows up in the pause after someone asks a question. In "All good" becoming the default response even when circumstances are anything but good.

Sometimes fear is a leader's sigh at the wrong moment. Sarcasm delivered as humor but received as a warning. Leaders don't always realize how much weight their subtle reactions carry. A comment that would be harmless from a peer can feel like a verdict coming from an authority figure.

That's why psychological safety matters. It's not about comfort. It's about whether people can tell the truth without first calculating the emotional cost.

Harvard researcher Amy Edmondson, who's studied psychological safety for decades, describes it as a shared belief that the team is safe for interpersonal risk-taking. In everyday language, it means people feel safe enough to ask questions, offer ideas, admit mistakes, challenge decisions, and say what needs to be said—even when it's uncomfortable.

Psychological safety gets misunderstood because it sounds gentle. It isn't. It's a performance condition.

Psychological Safety:

- It is not comfort.

- It is not lowered standards.

- It is not avoiding hard conversations.

- It is not protecting people from consequences.

- It is not "nice" leadership dressed up as culture.

- It is not the absence of pressure—it's the absence of humiliation.

- It is the ability to tell the truth early—before small problems become expensive ones.

- It is the freedom to say, "I'm not sure," without losing standing.

- It is candor with accountability: you can speak honestly, and you still own the outcome.

When safety is present, feedback lands as information, not a verdict. Standards stay high because learning speeds up. Teams correct, adapt, and recover faster. When safety is absent, people don't stop making mistakes—they stop surfacing them. That's not professionalism. That's risk management. And it's always slower than the truth.

A psychologically safe team is easy to recognize. People speak candidly. They disagree without the room going cold. They ask honest questions without apologizing. Ideas move around freely.

And then there are the other teams. The ones where everyone performs professionalism—smiling, nodding, harmonizing agreement for an audience that doesn't exist. Step into the hallway afterward, and you'll hear the sentence that quietly undermines everything: "I didn't say what I was thinking. It wasn't worth the fallout."

Google once studied what makes teams thrive (they called it Project Aristotle) and found a major driver of performance: psychological safety—not tenure, intelligence, or credentials. Safety speeds learning, adaptation, and recovery. Without it, teams shrink, information gets filtered, and leaders don't realize the damage until missed opportunities and unpleasant surprises start stacking up.

When people feel threatened—emotionally, professionally, or relationally—their brains don't move toward creativity. They move toward self-protection. Instead of scanning for possibilities, people scan the leader's reactions like a weather forecast, watching for signs of an approaching storm.

I learned this the hard way.

A young team member—let's call him Matthew—made a small mistake on a big day. Nothing unethical. Nothing irreversible. Just a human misstep under pressure. I was carrying more than I should have been, and in a moment I wish I could redo, I responded too quickly and too sharply.

The change in him was immediate and quiet. His shoulders tightened. His expression dimmed. Over the next few weeks, I watched him withdraw. He asked fewer questions. Offered fewer ideas. Took fewer risks. Not because he stopped caring, but because I unintentionally taught him that mistakes were unsafe around me.

That wasn't his failure. It was mine. Psychological safety can take months to build, but it can crack in seconds.

And here's the uncomfortable truth: many leaders say they want honesty, but they're only comfortable with honesty when it arrives gently, politely, and wrapped in affirmation. Real honesty is messier. It says, "This isn't working." It says, "I don't understand what you want." It says, "We're pretending this is fine, and it's not." Psychological safety doesn't just invite that honesty—it trains leaders to receive it without punishing the person who offered it.

Leaders who can handle truth get more of it; leaders who react defensively train their teams to bring them less.

So, build safety through patterns, not proclamations. Not through speeches about open communication. Not through posters on the wall. Build safety by responding well when it matters.

In my experience, it grows when leaders practice a few consistent habits:

- **Model humanity**—not performative vulnerability, but the simple willingness to say, "I missed that," or "I don't know yet," or "I need your perspective."

- **Reward initiative**, even when execution isn't perfect, signaling that effort and learning matter.

- **Invite pushback** and then listen long enough to hear it without defending yourself.

- **Respond thoughtfully** rather than impulsively, remembering that your tone sets the emotional tone of the room.

When something goes wrong, debrief without assigning blame and prioritize learning over punishment.

Every organization has a Blamethrower—the person who appears the moment something goes wrong, already holding a narrative that keeps them spotless while someone else gets scorched. Blamethrowers often believe they're protecting standards, but what they're really protecting is silence. People stop volunteering information around them. They stop raising issues early. They stop addressing problems while they are still small.

The opposite of a blamethrower is a mirror.

A mirror asks, "What part did I play in this?" Mirrors don't remove accountability; they deepen it. They create environments where people can be honest without needing armor. When leaders choose to be mirrors, the air in the room changes. People speak sooner, issues surface earlier, and ideas arrive less filtered. Mistakes become information instead of shame.

Psychological safety doesn't eliminate fear. Fear arises whenever the work matters. New responsibility brings uncertainty, new ideas bring exposure, and honest conversations bring discomfort. But when safety is present, fear no longer functions as a stop sign. It becomes background noise—the normal tension of doing meaningful work—rather than a threat to one's standing or identity.

This is why safety enables empowerment. Empowerment requires risk.

So, here's the question to sit with—not as theory, but as a mirror for your own leadership:

When someone brings you bad news, do they leave the conversation feeling smaller—or stronger?

Your answer is shaping the culture in real time. It's either giving empowerment oxygen—or quietly suffocating it.

Chapter 8 – Communicating for Empowerment

If I could give every leader a simple reminder—something small enough to fit on a sticky note but strong enough to change the temperature in a room—I'd give you a four-word question. Nothing poetic. Nothing elaborate. Nothing that requires a three-hour workshop and a laminated handout.

Just this:

"What do you think?"

Those four words don't shout. They don't posture. They don't come with leadership jargon or a dramatic soundtrack. But when they're offered sincerely—without a hidden test buried inside, without an agenda disguised as curiosity, without you already knowing the answer you hope to hear—they do something almost immediate. The room becomes slightly less hierarchical and slightly more human. People sit up straighter, not because they fear judgment, but because they realize you invited them into the conversation in a meaningful way.

It's strange how much weight those words carry when people have gone a long time without hearing them.

They tell someone, sometimes for the first time in a long time, "You're not just here to execute. You're here to think. And your thinking matters."

Most leaders don't set out to silence their teams. They read the books. They attend the conferences. They subscribe to podcasts hosted by people who sound like they were born wearing a blazer. Leaders collect tools, phrases, and frameworks. But the day-to-day pace sets in—deadlines, decisions, "urgent" requests dressed up as emergencies— and the simplest, most empowering tool gets neglected: language that invites people into ownership rather than pushing them into compliance.

Because words don't merely convey information, they create atmosphere. They shape the emotional conditions in which people work. A careless comment can deflate confidence with surprising speed—like shrinking a wool sweater to toddler size with one careless wash cycle. (I'm not saying this happened to me. I'm saying if it happened to me, I'm still not over it.) Conversely, an intentional shift in how you speak can create space for courage, creativity, and contribution. Most teams already carry those items; they just need language that encourages them to come out of hiding.

Empowering communication isn't poetic or dramatic. It isn't about speeches or slogans. It's simply the practice of talking with people instead of at them. It's the steady movement away from control and toward collaboration. And one of the easiest ways to notice the difference is to pay attention to the language we use without thinking— especially in moments when we're busy, stressed, or trying to move fast.

Here's a simple contrast. Yes, it's a chart. And yes, sometimes charts tell the truth with a blunt honesty that paragraphs politely avoid.

Disempowering	**Empowering**
"Just do it this way."	"Here's the goal—how would you approach it?"
"You wouldn't understand."	"Let me walk you through the why."

Disempowering	**Empowering**
"I'll handle it."	"You can own this—what support helps?"
"That's not your job."	"Not yet—but let's talk about growing into it."

One column communicates control.

The other communicates trust.

Teams feel that difference immediately. Empowering language creates openings for people to think, not just comply. It communicates belief long before belief ever becomes a formal transfer of responsibility. And it's one of the quiet ironies of leadership: people often rise faster when we stop trying to convince them of their potential and start speaking to them as if they already possess it.

I once worked with a manager—let's call him Kevin—who couldn't understand why his team depended on him for every decision. He felt trapped. He was always "needed," always being pulled into questions that, frankly, adults with job titles and fully functional frontal lobes should have been able to answer. He told me, with genuine frustration, "I've built them up. I coach them. I tell them I trust them. Why do they keep bringing everything to me?"

So I shadowed him for a day.

The answer didn't require much detective work. Kevin filled every conversation so completely that there was no oxygen left for anyone else to think. His meetings were monologues with hydration breaks. Not because he was arrogant or indifferent. He was simply trying to be helpful, clear, and keep things moving. However, his helpfulness had a side effect: it trained the team to wait for his input rather than to think independently.

I suggested an experiment that seemed almost trivial.

"Try speaking last," I said.

He looked at me the way people look at their dentist right before the drill comes out—suspicious, slightly betrayed, but willing to cooperate if it means long-term health. He agreed to try it. And yes, the first attempt was awkward. The silence was so thick that someone coughed to ensure the room still had oxygen.

But eventually, the silence softened. A few ideas surfaced. Then a few more. People started doing what they hadn't done in a long time: thinking out loud. The team filled the space Kevin had unintentionally occupied with their own perspectives.

Afterward, he leaned back in his chair and said something that stuck with him—and with me.

"Turns out my talking was the loudest barrier to their thinking."

That's the leadership sentence that should be printed on a mug, except then we'd all become the leaders we roll our eyes at. So maybe keep it in your pocket instead.

Empowering communication doesn't always begin with speaking. Sometimes it begins with restraint. Making room, not noise. There's a version of leadership where the leader believes their job is to have the answer quickly and confidently. And if someone brings them a problem, the leader feels the familiar tug to solve it on the spot. Solving feels helpful—efficient, even responsible.

But leadership isn't about becoming a walking encyclopedia of correct answers. Leadership is the slow, intentional work of shaping thinkers.

So, when someone brings you a problem, try offering questions that help them find the answer rather than supplying it yourself. Not interrogations. Not "gotcha" questions. Real questions that communicate belief.

"What options have you considered?"

"Where do you see the pressure points?"

"What feels like the next best step?"

"If our roles were reversed, how might you approach it?"

Every time you respond with a thoughtful question instead of a quick solution, you signal trust in their thinking. You build decision-making muscles. You teach them that you value their perspective, not just their output. And over time—slowly, almost quietly—people begin arriving with proposals instead of problems.

That shift alone can change a leader's workload, a team's momentum, and a culture's sense of ownership. It takes you out of the role of "final stop on the problem train" and places you where you belong: guiding direction, shaping judgment, strengthening people.

Now, there's a danger here, and it's worth naming. Leaders sometimes hear "ask more questions" and end up turning it into "be vague." Empowering communication isn't vague encouragement. It isn't tossing someone into uncertainty and calling it growth. People can't meaningfully contribute if they don't understand what success looks like. If the destination is foggy, asking "What do you think?" doesn't feel empowering—it feels like you handed them a map with no landmarks and said, "Good luck. Let's circle back when you're done."

Clarity matters. Not the clarity that arrives as a 47-slide deck, a manifesto, or a three-page email with the subject line "Quick Thought." Real clarity is simpler than that. It's the steady, grounded articulation of what matters and why it matters. It's naming the goal in a way that feels accessible, then trusting people with creative freedom inside that goal.

I remember a nurse once asking me, "Why do we do it like this?" and, for a split second, I felt tempted to use the classic leader reply: "Because that's the process." Quick and efficient—and completely dead-ending. The verbal equivalent of closing a door while smiling.

Instead, I slowed down and walked her through the reasoning—patient experience, safety protocols, consistency, how small habits ripple outward into trust. She listened, nodded, and then said, almost thoughtfully, "If that's the goal, we could enhance it even more if…"

And what followed was a smarter approach than the one we were using.

That moment was a reminder: explaining the "why" doesn't weaken authority. It strengthens alignment. It transforms compliance into contribution. It invites people to build something with you rather than merely carrying out a task you assigned.

Language also reveals what you reward. If you praise only outcomes, people will pursue whatever produces the fastest win. But if you acknowledge curiosity, initiative, and courage, people begin chasing growth. They begin to pay attention not only to what they have achieved but also to how they arrived there. They begin to recognize themselves as participants in progress rather than as task performers.

"I love your initiative."

"The idea didn't work, but the risk you took matters."

"Thanks for catching that early."

"I'm proud of the creativity you brought to this."

Those are small sentences. Gentle, even. But they collect over time. They tell people that effort matters. Learning matters. The process isn't just tolerated—it's valued. And praise offered this way doesn't inflate ego; it strengthens identity. It helps people understand not only what they did well, but who they are becoming.

As confidence grows, psychological ownership begins forming. Ownership rarely arrives from a command; it grows from participation. When someone has shaped the work, even in small ways, they move differently inside it. They stop treating assignments like obligations and start treating them like opportunities. And sometimes that shift begins with nothing more than a subtle language adjustment.

"I need this done by Friday" becomes "Can you own this by Friday?"

"We have to fix this" becomes "What's our best move here?"

"We can't do that" becomes "What would make that possible?"

These aren't tricks. They are an invitation to ownership in shared responsibility. People step toward work they feel connected to, and language is often the thread that binds them to it.

While we're here, we should address one of the more persistent leadership habits of the digital age: the Reply All Affliction. Leaders sometimes copy 10 people on an email, not because it's necessary, but because something inside them isn't fully ready to trust that a decision can live quietly between two humans without the electronic equivalent of an audience. It's rarely malicious. It's usually anxiety dressed in professionalism.

Empowering communication doesn't broadcast unnecessarily. It brings clarity without performing it. It brightens the situation without illuminating everyone involved. Sometimes empowerment sounds like, "You two decide and let me know what you choose," not "I'm looping in the entire organization so we can all breathe the same air together."

The deeper point is this: communication that empowers has a rhythm. You name the direction. You create space for dialogue. Through dialogue, discovery occurs— discovery in the work and in people. Leaders who skip that middle step often wonder why their teams don't feel a sense of ownership. The answer is painfully simple: empowerment lives in the dialogue.

But none of this matters if you're not willing to listen. And I don't mean the distracted nod while your eyes drift toward a screen, or the polite "mm-hmm" that says, "I'm here, but my brain is in three other meetings." I mean, listening that arrives in the room and says, "Your voice is here, and so am I."

There's a paradox in leadership that reveals itself over time: the more you listen, the less you need to manage. People who feel heard rarely need to be herded. They calibrate themselves. They contribute more willingly. They bring solutions with fewer prompting questions. Many people treat listening as something soft, but it's one of the most strategically powerful moves a leader can make, because it draws out intelligence you didn't have access to when you were doing all the talking.

And this is where the magic is—not dramatic magic, not leadership-theatre magic, but real, everyday transformation. Empowering communication isn't about being eloquent. It's about intention. It's speaking in a way that honors the intelligence of the people around you. It's asking questions that strengthen rather than shrink. It's offering clarity that doesn't confine but instead gives shape to possibility. It's using your position not as a platform for your answers, but as a way to elevate other people's thinking.

Words build worlds. Every conversation is a construction—laying beams of clarity, opening windows of possibility, strengthening the foundation beneath the work you're asking people to carry.

So, speak as if you are building something that will outlast the meeting. Ask questions that invite contribution. Make space with your silence. Explain the "why" when it matters.

Praise courage, not just polish. And listen in a way that reminds people their voice belongs in the room.

Empowering communication isn't ultimately about being right.

It's about helping other people discover their capacity—the capacity that grows when leaders talk a little less, listen a little more, and treat every conversation as an invitation to rise.

As we move forward, we'll take this one step deeper. Because language and listening create the conditions for ownership—but conditions alone aren't the full story. At some point, empowerment becomes structural. It becomes evident in how decisions are made, how work is designed, and how responsibility is carried. We'll get there. For now, start here:

"What do you think?"

Say it like you mean it. Then make room for the answer.

Operating Notes — Put This into Practice

This week, let your communication transfer ownership—ask "What do you think?" and make room for their judgment to lead.

Actions

- Choose one outcome to hand off: name the result, then explicitly transfer responsibility + authority + support (all three).

- Make the destination clear: write one short paragraph that answers, "What does winning look like?" (not a deck, not a manifesto).

- Ask the four-word question daily: "What do you think?" Ask it without a hidden test and without steering it toward your preferred answer.

- Speak last once per day: create space for others to think out loud before your authority fills the room.

- Reward initiative—even when imperfect: notice the effort and learning, then help refine execution without humiliation.

- Invite pushback on purpose: in your next meeting, ask, "What are we missing?" and sit in the silence long enough to hear a real answer.

Scripts (use them verbatim if you want)

1. **Ownership invitation**

   "What do you think? I'm not grading you—I want your judgment. Bring me a recommendation, not just an update."

2. **Safety + standards (not softness)**

   "I want the truth early. You won't get punished for raising it. We'll learn fast and keep the standard high."

Watch-fors

- Leashership: you hand out empowerment language, then quietly rewrite the work or reclaim decisions "just this once."

- Freedom without orientation: you say "use your judgment," but never clarify what judgment applies to.

- Micro-signals that shut truth down: the sigh, the eyebrow, the sarcasm that lands like a warning.

Reflection questions

- Where do I say "run with it" but still keep the wheel in my hands?

- Do people bring me proposals—or only problems and permission requests?

- When someone disagrees, does the room get colder—or clearer?

Part IV: Autonomy

Autonomy is where teams either scale—or stall. This part answers the question: **how do you create freedom that doesn't erode standards?** You'll design decision clarity and practice accountability that protects the standard without hovering.

Watch for autonomy without guardrails, accountability used as surveillance, and leaders overfunctioning "just to be safe."

This is the shift from being the bottleneck to building a system that carries the work.

Chapter 9 – Defining True Autonomy

I've watched a particular moment in leadership repeat itself often enough that it's become familiar in the way certain stories always are. A leader stands before their team, energized and sincere, and talks about autonomy as ownership. About wanting people to think and act without waiting for someone to tell them what to do. The idea lands well, because it always does. Autonomy sounds like trust. It sounds like progress. It sounds like the leadership we most want to believe we're practicing. Heads nod. The room feels lighter. And in that moment, everything feels aligned.

Then someone actually believes the leader.

A day or two later, a team member makes a unilateral decision. They solve a problem quietly. They move forward instead of waiting. And something subtle happens inside the leader—no visible reaction, no correction—just a quick internal recalibration. The pause lasts a fraction of a second, but it's enough. Enough to reveal the tension most leaders don't say out loud: autonomy is far easier to admire than it is to live with. Independent thinking sounds noble in theory, but it can feel unsettling in practice.

This is where the paradox of autonomy lives. Leaders often say they want autonomy, but what they're really hoping for is predictability with enthusiasm. They want initiatives that mirror their instincts, decisions that stay inside their comfort zone, and outcomes that still feel familiar—even when they weren't personally involved. Autonomy rarely arrives that way. It brings different perspectives, different priorities, sometimes different conclusions. And when that happens, autonomy presses on more than workflow—it presses on control, identity, and the quiet reassurance that comes from being the final authority.

Autonomy can't be reduced to "control with nicer language." It's also more than delegation dressed up as trust. Autonomy happens when someone understands the mission well enough to act without having to borrow your judgment every time. That's why it's revealing. It doesn't diminish leadership; it exposes it. It shows whether expectations were clear enough to be internalized, whether development took root, and whether trust extends beyond words to real responsibility. Autonomy doesn't remove the need for leadership—it reshapes it.

I often think about autonomy the same way I think about teaching someone to drive. At the beginning, every nerve is engaged. Your hands hover near the wheel. Your foot presses an imaginary brake. Your body convinces you disaster is always one decision away. But slowly, as the person learns the rules, gains rhythm, and starts anticipating rather than reacting, something changes within you as well. You loosen your grip as their reliability increases. Your role shifts from controlling every turn to trusting what you helped build. That moment—when you finally unclench—is the heart of autonomy.

I once watched a leader introduce autonomy with genuine enthusiasm and almost no preparation. He announced, "You all have complete freedom now," and meant it. His intent was real. The issue was the absence of orientation. People were suddenly free without knowing what they were free to decide, design, or change. Freedom without clarity doesn't feel liberating—it feels disorienting.

Autonomy grows inside shared understanding: clear outcomes, shared priorities, and alignment about what matters. Leaders define the destination well enough that people can choose their own path without drifting off course. When that foundation is missing, autonomy turns into hesitation or chaos. When it's present, autonomy no longer needs to be announced. It emerges naturally.

That's why autonomy always rests on three conditions:

1. **Clarity** about the outcome

2. **Competence** to act

3. **Confidence** that someone trusts you to try.

Remove any one of those, and autonomy collapses. But when all three are present, autonomy shows up in ways that look almost ordinary.

A helpful boundary here: autonomy answers "who decides and acts," while accountability answers "how we know we're winning—and what we do when we're not." Autonomy gives people latitude; accountability gives that latitude direction. Pair them, and you get speed without chaos.

I observed this in a surgical unit experiencing long turnover times. Everyone was busy. Everyone was involved. And yet nothing improved, because no one truly owned the process—no one, except Theresa.

Theresa wasn't a manager. She didn't carry formal authority. However, she understood the unit's rhythm and was deeply committed to the patient experience. She reviewed weeks of patterns and observed that the delays weren't caused by volume but by unpredictability. She designed a unified rounding schedule, constructed a simple communication board, and proposed a trial run. Leadership approved it. Turnover times dropped. Stress eased. Patients noticed. When asked how she came up with the plan, Theresa simply said, "Patients deserved better. And so did we."

That was autonomy in action—someone identifying a gap, trusting their judgment, and acting within the mission instead of waiting for permission.

Autonomy often looks like that. Quiet. Ordinary. Almost unremarkable at first glance. It doesn't announce itself. It shows up when someone believes they're allowed to act.

I've seen it in small moments too—a barista explaining the flow of the space to a new hire and then stepping aside, trusting them to move within it. No hovering. No constant correction. Just clarity paired with belief. Within an hour, the new employee moves with confidence, not because they're gifted but because someone created conditions where thinking was welcome.

One reason autonomy feels both inspiring and intimidating is that it rarely arrives all at once. Leaders treat it like a switch, but autonomy is more like taking off training wheels. Remove them before someone has balance, and they crash—then you conclude they weren't ready. Leave them on forever, and they never learn to ride. But remove them in stages, and the rider becomes stable.

This is where many leaders struggle—not because they dislike autonomy as an idea, but because letting go challenges the parts of leadership that feel validating. Being the answer-holder feels useful. Being the decision-maker feels competent. Autonomy asks leaders to trade being needed for being effective.

That trade is uncomfortable. It forces you to consider the possibility that someone else might make a better decision than you would. Autonomy reframes that as success. Leadership shifts from personal excellence to collective capacity. Autonomy is proximity without pressure. When people know you're available—without hovering—they take risks with steadier hands. Over time, standards become internal rather than enforced. Excellence no longer requires supervision because it has been absorbed.

When autonomy is present, teams move differently. Meetings feel lighter. Problems surface earlier. Ideas emerge from places leaders would never have seen on their own. Leadership distributes itself—not through authority, but through ownership.

When autonomy is absent, even capable people shrink. They wait. They check. They hesitate—not because they lack ability, but because the environment has never given them the confidence that their ability is valued.

In the chapters ahead, we'll look at what makes autonomy sustainable, how leaders create clarity, build capability, and hold accountability without pulling control back into their own hands. But autonomy has to be real. If it only exists when people make the decisions you would've made, it isn't autonomy, it's permission.

Before you turn the page, do a quick audit:

- Where are you asking for ownership while still needing to agree with the path?

- Where have you left the outcome vague, forcing people to borrow your judgment?

- Who is ready for more latitude—if you'll stop hovering long enough for them to use it?

Autonomy is the moment leadership stops being the bottleneck and becomes the multiplier.

Chapter 10 – Building Systems for Autonomy

Whenever the conversation turns toward systems, you can almost feel something shift in the room. People settle back in their chairs slightly, as if bracing for a discussion about bureaucracy, approvals, or processes no one actually likes but everyone has learned to tolerate. Systems carry baggage. Many of us have worked within structures that were confusing, rigid, or clearly designed for a different version of the organization than the one we face today. So when leaders say the word "systems," people picture binders no one opens, workflows no one fully understands, and approval chains that seem to exist mainly to slow things down.

Then, often in the same breath, leaders talk about autonomy. And suddenly a different concern surfaces. Autonomy can seem energizing until someone uses it in a way the leader wouldn't have chosen. Until a decision appears that wasn't pre-approved. Until something moves faster than expected. What people feel in that moment isn't chaos—it's tension. The tension of two ideas we learned to hold apart: structure and freedom.

One important caveat—especially in regulated work: autonomy is never permission to improvise around non-negotiables. Your team can own decisions, but the rails are fixed: safety, law, privacy, ethics, scope-of-practice, and the promises you've made to patients or customers. When those rails are unclear, people either freeze or gamble—neither is autonomy. So name the non-negotiables plainly, and pair them with constraints that keep judgment aligned: budget limits, required approvals, escalation triggers, and what "stop the line" looks like.

A simple script works: "You own the decision inside these boundaries. If it touches safety, compliance, privacy, or crosses $_____ / changes the customer promise, escalate immediately." Clear constraints don't shrink autonomy. They make it usable.

Systems and autonomy are partners. Autonomy does not happen in the absence of structure. It happens because of it.

Most leaders don't realize this until autonomy begins to break down. Not loudly. Not rebelliously. Quietly.

Decisions stall. Initiative slows. People start asking for permission again, not because they want control, but because they're unsure where authority actually lies. Decisions and work start climbing the organizational chart rather than moving across it. Leaders feel busier than ever, while simultaneously wondering why their teams seem hesitant to act.

What's often missing isn't motivation or trust. It's Decision Architecture.

By Decision Architecture, I mean the deliberate design of who decides what, within which boundaries, and when a decision escalates—so ownership doesn't leak upward by default.

Every organization has a decision system, whether it exists by design or by default. Decisions either flow clearly, or they leak upward. They either live close to the work or drift toward whoever feels safest holding them. And when decision ownership is unclear, autonomy doesn't disappear—it collapses inward. People default to caution. They wait. They check. They loop others in "to be safe." Not because they lack judgment, but because the system never told them where judgment was expected to reside.

I once worked with a nonprofit whose mission could move you within minutes. The work mattered deeply. The people cared. And yet everything felt heavier than it should have. Volunteers hesitated before acting. Staff members improvised constantly, unsure whether their choices would later be questioned. And nearly every decision—large or small—found its way back to the director's desk. She wasn't controlling. She was overwhelmed. The system had trained everyone to treat her as the final checkpoint because no one else knew where decisions were supposed to land.

After a particularly chaotic event, a young coordinator named Sofia said something so gently that it almost went unnoticed. "We don't need more effort," she said. "We need a way of working that doesn't depend on one person remembering everything." It wasn't criticism. It was clarity.

What followed wasn't a cultural reset or an inspirational speech. It was structural work. The team mapped how decisions were made—not how they believed they were made. They noticed that ownership was fuzzy. Decisions floated. People acted, but without clear authority. Others waited, afraid of overstepping. The director wasn't a bottleneck because she wanted to be; she was a bottleneck because the system had nowhere else for decisions to go.

When we rebuilt their approach, we didn't start with empowerment language. We started with decision clarity.

Who decides what? Which decisions belong to roles rather than to people? Which decisions require escalation, and which should never? We created simple boundaries, not heavy rules. Almost immediately, the work changed. People stopped checking as often. The director stopped hovering. Responsibility distributed itself naturally once the structure made it possible.

This is one of the most misunderstood truths about autonomy: people don't need permission to act as much as they need certainty about where they're allowed to act.

Autonomy collapses fastest in environments where decision-making is implied rather than defined. Where leaders say, "Use your judgment," but never clarify what judgment applies to. When escalation paths are informal, and authority is emotional rather than structural, autonomy feels risky because no one knows which invisible boundary might be crossed.

Healthy systems remove that uncertainty. They make decision ownership visible. They tell people, without speeches or slogans, "This is yours to decide. This is where support lives. This is when escalation helps rather than hurts."

You can see this play out clearly in organizations where autonomy is lived rather than advertised. People don't ask permission for routine decisions because the system has already answered the question. They don't hesitate to act because everyone knows the boundaries. When escalation happens, it feels like collaboration, not correction.

Airbnb—an online marketplace where people rent out homes and rooms to travelers—recognized this early in its growth. With hosts worldwide offering wildly different experiences, they needed quality without sacrificing individuality. Instead of controlling every decision, they studied where decisions mattered most and where freedom added value. They created clear standards for safety, cleanliness, and communication, and then stepped back. Hosts didn't become reckless. They became more thoughtful. The system carried the fundamentals so people could invest creativity where it counted.

I observed the same pattern in a healthcare clinic experiencing patient flow challenges. Wait times were long. Stress was constant. Leadership assumed the issue was staffing or scheduling. But the deeper problem was decision paralysis. No one knew who could change the flow once the day started.

Then one medical assistant, Jordan, experimented with rooming patients by visit type rather than by arrival time. It worked. Not because he was rebellious, but because the system allowed experimentation without fear. Leadership recognized the improvement and formalized a simple guideline: small operational decisions could be tested immediately, provided they didn't violate safety or compliance.

That single shift didn't create chaos. It created momentum. The clinic improved week by week, not because leaders made every decision, but because the system told people where decisions belonged.

This is the power of Decision Architecture. When systems clarify decision ownership, leaders cease to be the center of motion and become the designers of motion. Autonomy ceases to feel like a gamble and instead becomes a matter of alignment.

A useful question for leaders isn't, "Do we trust our people?" Rather, it's, "Do our systems tell people what they're trusted to decide?"

If decisions stall when one person is absent, the system is broken. If people wait because they're unsure whether they're allowed to act, the system is broken. If initiative feels risky rather than responsible, the system is broken. And fixing it doesn't require more motivation—it requires clearer structure.

Good systems behave like scaffolding. They support the work as it grows, distributing weight so no one carries too much alone. When you design scaffolding well, you hardly notice it. When it's missing, everything wobbles.

Designing systems this way is not administrative work. It is leadership work. It says to people, "You don't have to guess. You don't have to check every step. You don't have to carry the whole thing in your head." Systems function as shared memory, preserving clarity even as people change.

When systems and autonomy align—when decision ownership is clear, boundaries are visible, and escalation is purposeful—the atmosphere changes. People move with steadiness. Decisions surface earlier. Problems get solved closer to their source. Leadership influence expands because it no longer depends on presence.

And that's the point: empowerment can start as a conversation, but autonomy survives through structure. Systems don't replace leadership; they carry it forward. They protect good judgment from being trapped inside one person's head. They turn trust into something people can actually use.

If you want a quick diagnostic, don't start with how your team feels. Start with what happens when the day gets messy. When a leader is out. When the decision is uncomfortable. When the answer isn't obvious. In those moments, your real system appears. People either act with confidence or reach upward for safety.

So, run this test on your environment:

- Where do decisions regularly climb the org chart that should live closer to the work?

- Where are the boundaries implied instead of stated, forcing people to guess what "good judgment" means?

- Where does escalation feel like getting in trouble instead of getting help?

In the next chapter, we'll make this tangible—how to define decision lanes, build escalation triggers, and create simple guardrails to keep autonomy from drifting. Because the goal isn't more process. It's less guessing.

A healthy system doesn't feel like a cage. It feels like traction.
And traction is what lets people rise—without needing you to hold the wheel.

Chapter 11 – Accountability

Every leader eventually learns leadership has moments that feel like a ridgeline: one wrong step and everything shifts. Lean too far toward control, and you slowly drain your team's energy, shrinking initiative until capable people begin waiting for someone to tell them what to do. Lean too far toward freedom without structure, and you invite confusion, inconsistency, and work that feels unpredictable rather than empowered. Most leaders don't wobble because they're careless; they wobble because they care deeply and are trying to protect outcomes without fully trusting the conditions they've created. What steadies that balance isn't intensity or charisma. It's accountability—clear and shared.

Autonomy and accountability aren't opposites—they're the pair that makes ownership work. Autonomy answers: **Who makes the call?** Accountability answers: **What does**

"good" look like, and how will we know? Clear outcomes. Clear standards. A short feedback loop.

Without autonomy, decisions slow down, and people disengage. Without accountability, decisions scatter and quality drifts. In regulated environments, accountability keeps the non-negotiables real, while autonomy keeps work moving.

But accountability gets misunderstood, and that's where leaders get into trouble. Not the clipboard version—the one that looks like diligence but feels like surveillance. Not the "copy half the organization" version that proves someone is watching. Real accountability is calmer. It's shared expectations, visible ownership, and follow-through. When it's healthy, it doesn't feel like pressure closing in; it feels like purpose pulling people forward. And when leaders confuse accountability with hovering, micromanagement wears a convincing disguise.

Many leaders struggle here because micromanagement wears a convincing disguise. It often presents itself as care. Leaders rewrite someone's work "to help." They insert themselves into decisions "to stay aligned." They ask for constant updates "to be sure." None of it is malicious. Most of it stems from a sincere desire to prevent errors and protect individuals from failure. But over time, that posture teaches a dangerous lesson: thinking is optional, initiative is risky, and leadership belongs to someone else. Micromanagement doesn't raise standards; it erodes confidence. It doesn't accelerate performance; it trains people to wait.

The difference between micromanagement and accountability becomes clear once you feel it.

Micromanagement tries to control the process. Accountability defines outcomes and relies on people to achieve them. Micromanagement is driven by anxiety about potential errors. Accountability is anchored in clarity about what matters. One produces compliance. The other produces commitment.

I learned this early in my career during the launch of a new urgent care practice. From the outside, everything looked promising—new space, energized staff, big expectations. Internally, we lived in what I now recognize as the land of *almost*. The supply room was almost stocked. Charts were almost completed. Labs were almost processed correctly. Nobody was lazy or incompetent. We simply lacked shared ownership, and *almost* became the ceiling we kept hitting.

Eventually, we realized effort wasn't the problem. Ambiguity was. So instead of tightening control, we simplified responsibility. Each role defined a clear promise to the patient—one outcome they fully owned. The front desk owned accurate registration. Medical assistants owned dependable rooming. Providers owned timely documentation. And leadership owned clearing obstacles rather than creating them. We paired those promises with a brief weekly rhythm in which participants shared how they delivered on their promise and what support they needed next. Within weeks, the tone shifted. Errors dropped. Flow improved. People stood a little taller, not because they were being monitored, but because they knew exactly what winning looked like.

One medical assistant said something I've never forgotten: "Accountability feels heavy until you taste what it's like to win." That sentence captures the heart of accountability. It isn't meant to burden people; it's meant to aim them.

At its core, accountability rests on three elements working together:

1. **Clarity**: They know what success looks like

2. **Ownership**: They own their contribution

3. **Feedback**: They receive feedback soon enough to adjust.

Remove any one, and accountability collapses. When clarity, ownership, or feedback is missing, people start guessing, deflecting, and drifting. Leaders sometimes try to compensate by repeating expectations louder or more often, but reminders without ownership quickly become background noise.

Handled well, autonomy strengthens accountability by reconnecting effort to outcome. When people feel pride in seeing their work matter, motivation becomes intrinsic rather than extrinsic.

I've led many leaders who understood this instinctively. Before launching any major initiative, they convened the team for a brief alignment discussion. They clarified what success entailed, who was responsible for which decisions, and how progress would be evaluated without micromanagement. Then they stepped back—not far enough for people to feel abandoned, but far enough for them to lead. The project, more often than not, finished early, not because they worked harder, but because ambiguity wasn't slowing anyone down.

Visibility plays a critical role here. Many leaders believe accountability means chasing updates, but chasing creates tension and inefficiency. Healthier accountability comes from making progress visible without making people defensive. Shared dashboards, short stand-ups, or simple boards allow everyone to see where things stand without interrogation. The tone shifts from "I'm checking on you" to "we're looking at this together."

I've seen what happens when visibility turns into surveillance all too often. In one organization I was with, employees were required to submit nightly activity reports and then defend them in daily meetings. People spent more time proving they worked than actually working. I've never experienced a morale drop as fast in my career, including my own. And guess what – results never improved.

By contrast, I had a leader do the opposite: he replaced daily check-ins with a shared scoreboard that the team updated themselves. Not surprisingly, within weeks, productivity rose—not because pressure increased, but because trust did. People owned their numbers instead of bracing to explain them. Oh, and morale never dropped; it improved.

Feedback completes the loop. Accountability is most effective when feedback is provided in real time rather than months later during a formal review. Small, timely adjustments prevent drift and sustain standards. Simple questions—"What's working? What's blocking you? What do you need from me?" I often do more to sustain accountability than any evaluation form ever will.

What often goes unspoken is that weak accountability punishes the wrong people. High performers become frustrated when they carry more than their share, while others hide behind the ambiguity. Clear accountability is fair. It protects the people who care by ensuring their efforts are visible and their contributions matter.

If you want to assess accountability on your team, ask yourself a few questions:

- Do people know what great looks like?

- Do they know what they own?

- Do they get feedback soon enough to course-correct?

- Do you trust them to tell the truth about progress?

When the answer is yes, you're not managing—you're leading.

Because accountability, at its best, is not control. It's stewardship. It's the shared agreement that we will do what we've said because the work deserves our best, not because someone is watching. When leaders create that environment, people begin to hold themselves accountable with pride rather than under pressure.

That's when teams stop wobbling on the ridge and start moving forward with confidence, balance, and momentum.

And that's also where the next challenge appears: once ownership is real and accountability is shared, the question becomes how to raise the bar without squeezing the life out of the team. That's what Part V is about—***Excellence***.

Not perfection. Not "more oversight." Excellence as a repeatable standard: clear expectations, clean handoffs, tight feedback loops, and work that gets better because the team knows what "great" is and has the rhythm to keep reaching it—without you having to push every step.

Operating Notes — Put This into Practice

This week, hold the standard without hovering—build accountability that feels like stewardship, not surveillance.

Actions

- Map your decision architecture: list the 10 most common decisions in your area and write one line: who decides what (by role, not by personality).

- Draw three boundaries: what must be escalated (safety/compliance), what's spend-limited (budget), and what's locally owned (day-to-day operations).

- Make ownership visible: create a simple shared board/dashboard that shows progress on 3 outcomes without turning it into surveillance.

- Define a clear "role promise": for each key role, name the one outcome they fully own (the patient/customer promise).

- Replace chasing with rhythm: a brief weekly check-in. "What's working? What's blocking you? What do you need from me?"

- Run one low-risk experiment: invite a team member to test a process improvement inside the boundaries, then formalize what works.

Scripts (use them verbatim if you want)

1. **Decision clarity**

   "This decision lives with you. Here's what good looks like and the boundary you can't cross. If you hit that boundary, pull me in early."

2. **Accountability without micromanagement**

   "Let's look at progress together. I'm not checking to catch you—I'm checking so we learn fast. Tell me what you need to hit the standard."

Watch-fors

- Implied authority: decisions leak upward because no one is sure where action is allowed.

- Micromanagement in disguise: rewriting work "to help," constant updates "to be sure," and anxiety posing as diligence.

- Surveillance accountability: copying half the organization to prove someone is watching.

Reflection questions

- Where do decisions stall when one person is absent?

- Do our systems tell people what they're trusted to decide—or do they have to guess?

- Is escalation collaboration—or correction?

Part V: Excellence

Excellence isn't intensity. It's consistency that holds when no one is watching. This part answers: **what makes excellence durable, and what makes leadership last beyond you?** You'll build habits, culture, and rhythm that sustain performance under pressure and over time.

Watch for perfection masquerading as excellence, urgency becoming identity, and culture talk that never becomes daily practice.

This is where reframed leadership becomes legacy.

Chapter 12 – What Excellence Really Means

Most organizations talk about excellence like it's a personality trait—something a few high performers naturally possess. But in real life, "excellent" is usually just a label we apply after the fact, once results show up and we're proud of them. The trouble is that results can be produced in ways that don't last: through exhaustion, fear, heroic effort, or a leader who quietly carries the whole system on their back.

That's why this chapter matters. Excellence isn't the same as intensity. It isn't the same as speed. And it isn't the same as a team surviving another hard quarter. Excellence is what holds when no one is watching—when standards are clear, ownership is normal, and performance doesn't depend on one person's willpower.

Excellence is usually presented as something elevated and dramatic, a standard perched just out of reach, daring people to stretch until they either achieve it or exhaust themselves trying. In that version, excellence is defined by flawlessness, intensity, and continuous forward momentum. It sounds inspiring, but it often turns into image management—looking excellent instead of getting better.

The irony is that this framing doesn't produce better work; it produces anxiety, theater, and burnout. When excellence is treated as perfection, people don't rise to it. They brace against it. But when you strip away the theatrics, something much more human comes into view. Excellence is the steady choice to do the next right thing well, repeatedly, even when no one is watching. Excellence isn't loud. It isn't glamorous. It doesn't announce itself with awards or slogans.

I once watched this realization change the trajectory of a leader named Marcus. He was capable, driven, and well-liked, the person everyone assumed would succeed simply because success seemed to follow him. However, over time, the expectations accumulated. Small gaps went unspoken. Assumptions replaced clarity. And slowly, the weight of "being excellent" began to crush him. By the time we sat down to talk, he had already convinced himself he had failed. He entered the conversation prepared for correction, documentation, and perhaps an ending. What he didn't expect was for someone to ask him what story he was telling himself. When the words finally came, they weren't about metrics or outcomes; they were about worth. He felt exposed. Disappointed. Behind. He was measuring himself against a version of excellence that left no room for learning.

That conversation shifted when excellence shifted from proving to understanding. We laid everything out—not to assign blame, but to name reality. Gaps that had never been clarified. Systems that worked against him. Expectations that lived only in people's heads, nowhere else. As the fog lifted, something subtle but powerful happened. His posture changed. He stopped defending and started engaging. The clinic didn't improve because he became perfect—it improved because he became consistent. Because excellence, reframed properly, is not about avoiding mistakes; it's about responding to them with honesty, humility, and intention.

But excellence doesn't only reveal itself in leadership offices or turnaround moments. More often, it shows up quietly, carried by people whose names rarely appear on slides.

There was a woman named Elena who worked evening custodial shifts in a medical building I visited regularly. Most people never noticed her. She moved through hallways after clinics closed, resetting rooms for the next day. What caught my attention over time was something almost embarrassingly small: every morning, without fail, exam rooms felt calm when you walked into them. Supplies were placed the same way. Chairs were squared. Floors were clean without feeling sterile. Nothing flashy. Nothing that would ever earn a compliment.

One evening, I thanked her for her work and made an offhand comment about how consistent the building always felt. She smiled—not proudly, not defensively—and said, "I just try to leave it better for the first patient than it was for the last one."

That was it. No speech. No philosophy. Just a standard she carried with her every night.

No one told her to do that. No dashboard tracked it. No one applauded. But the effect was real. Providers started their day steadier. Patients entered rooms that conveyed care. Stress lowered in ways no metric ever captured. That's excellence—the kind that doesn't announce itself but changes the experience of everyone who follows.

This is the truth most leaders eventually learn: excellence grows from belief, not pressure. It requires clarity sturdy enough to guide decisions, consistency gentle enough to be sustained, and reflection honest enough to correct course without shame. When excellence is grounded in this way, mistakes become information rather than indictments. Progress matters more than polish. Direction matters more than speed. And people begin to move with a steadiness that intensity can never create.

Excellence, lived well, is incremental. It shows up in small adjustments that compound over time. A slightly better handoff. A clearer expectation. A more thoughtful conversation. These changes don't feel impressive in the moment, which is exactly why they work. They are human-sized. Sustainable. Repeating them doesn't require heroics, only attention. Over time, those small improvements reshape the entire culture, not through reinvention, but through refinement. Build excellence in layers, not leaps.

What often undermines excellence is the belief that it comes from urgency. Urgency looks productive, but it is fragile. It relies on adrenaline, and adrenaline eventually runs out. Excellence, by contrast, is durable. It lives in the ordinary rhythms of work, in the moments no one celebrates. I've watched teams chase excellence through intensity only to collapse under its weight. I've also watched teams reclaim excellence by doing something almost embarrassingly simple: slowing down just enough to notice where friction has formed and easing it with intention.

When you encounter a truly excellent team, you can sense it before you can explain it. There's a rhythm to how they operate, a quiet loop of observe, adjust, repeat. They don't chase perfection. They pursue better. They don't archive "best practices" and move on. They revisit their practices with curiosity and humility, asking what still serves the work and what no longer does. Excellence stays alive because it's practiced, not preserved.

This is why perfection is such a poor substitute for excellence.

Perfection insists on flawlessness and punishes deviation. Excellence invites growth and rewards honesty.

Perfection creates distance between people and standards. Excellence creates a connection between people and purpose.

Perfection imagines a destination.
Excellence commits to a direction.

One exhausts. The other endures.

If we left this conversation to move back into real life, I suspect the lingering thought would be: excellence feels lighter than perfection because it's anchored in meaning, not fear. People do excellent work when they understand why it matters, when they're allowed to learn in public, and when improvement is a shared pursuit. Excellence doesn't announce itself when everything goes right. It shows how people respond when things don't go as planned—in the willingness to adjust rather than defend, and the courage to choose better tomorrow.

So, trade pressure for the purpose. Trade flawless appearances for honest progress. Let excellence be what it was always meant to be—not a standard that hovers above people, but a path they can actually walk, together, one deliberate step at a time.

Chapter 13 – The Habits of Excellent Leaders

If I could take you behind the scenes of truly excellent leaders—not the ones chasing microphones or polishing the latest inspirational quote, but the ones people trust almost instinctively—you'd probably be surprised by how ordinary their days look. There's nothing cinematic about their routines. Nothing dramatic enough to trend or impressive enough to earn a place on a glossy list of "elite leadership rituals." Their days are steady. Predictable, even. And that's exactly the point.

There's an alignment to the way they move through the world. You notice it long before they speak. It shows up in how they enter a room—not to command attention, but to settle it. In the way their presence feels consistent, familiar, and reliable. They're the same person on Monday as they are on Thursday, regardless of how turbulent the week has been. They don't oscillate between leadership personas depending on stress levels or inbox volume. They don't swing from visionary to firefighter based on the moment's mood. Instead, they operate according to habits that anchor them in who they intend to be.

Those habits don't look impressive in isolation. Most of them wouldn't earn applause if announced out loud. They don't sparkle or shout. In fact, they hide in plain sight. But stacked together—day after day—they create something unmistakable. People say things like, "I think better when they're around," or "Things feel calmer when they're leading," or "I trust them without trying." What's almost ironic is that excellent leaders rarely think of themselves as exceptional. They don't carry intensity or superiority. They simply practice rhythms that keep stress, ego, urgency, and insecurity from becoming their default operating system.

I saw this clearly years ago while shadowing several leaders across a large organization. One stood out immediately, not because of charisma or credentials, but because his days looked unremarkable on paper. He didn't rush down hallways clutching papers like the building might collapse without him. He didn't sigh loudly or project an ambient sense of emergency. He didn't carry the frantic energy of someone convinced everything hinged on their personal involvement.

He had a rhythm. A gentle, predictable loop. He checked in with his team. Followed up on yesterday's commitments. Clarified today's priorities. Met with a few people. Walked the floor. Tied up loose ends. Went home on time.

That was it.

No theatrics. No manufactured urgency. No emotional whiplash disguised as passion. Just a leader who understood that steadiness is not a personality trait—it's a discipline.

And here's what struck me most: his team mirrored him. Turnover was low. Performance was consistently strong. Not because they were extraordinary, but because they weren't constantly recovering from volatility. New hires found their footing more quickly, not because the work was easy, but because the environment was sufficiently stable for learning. When challenges surfaced—as they always do—he didn't declare emergencies or launch into blame. He simply said, "Alright. Let's figure this out," in a tone that made even anxious people exhale.

When I finally asked him how he stayed so grounded, he said something that lodged itself in my thinking and never left: "If I don't build good habits on purpose, my stress will make decisions for me."

He was right. Stress doesn't choose clarity. It doesn't choose wisdom or alignment. Stress chooses urgency. Reactivity. Decisions that feel justified in the moment and regrettable in hindsight. Habits protect leaders from becoming the least grounded versions of themselves.

There are countless books about the routines of high performers. Still, when you strip away the noise, excellent leaders tend to live out the same few habits, not because a workshop assigned them to it, but because leadership itself nudged them in that direction over time.

Reflect

They build small pauses into their days—not dramatic retreats or hour-long reflection sessions, but simple moments to ask, "What did we learn from that?" Without reflection, leaders drift. They repeat patterns without noticing. They carry yesterday's confusion into tomorrow's decisions. A few minutes at the end of the day—what worked, what didn't, what matters next—can prevent weeks of unnecessary friction later. Reflection is like cleaning a windshield; you don't realize how blurry things were until you wipe it clear.

Listen

They listen differently, too. Not listening to reply or correct, but listening to understand. Something subtle shifts on a team when people feel genuinely heard. They stop performing and start participating. They stop guarding their thoughts and start offering them.

One leader I shadowed rarely spoke first in meetings. When I asked why, he said, "My voice has authority. If I speak too soon, I'll drown out truth without meaning to." His restraint created space for clarity—and for trust to grow without effort.

Focus

Excellent leaders also practice focus in a way that feels almost countercultural. They don't try to be everywhere or lead everything. They steward their attention deliberately. One leader I worked with kept a handwritten note taped to her monitor that read, "These are the only things I lead." She delegated, delayed, or declined anything outside that list. Her clarity became the team's clarity. Focus wasn't about doing more; it was about doing what mattered well enough to matter.

Gratitude

They practice gratitude intentionally, not as a personality quirk, but as a means of reinforcement. Gratitude may look soft at first glance, but it's leadership steel. It says, "I saw that," and "You matter," and "Keep going," all at once. And it's specific. Vague praise floats away. Specific appreciation sticks. It strengthens identity, not ego, and transforms feedback into partnership rather than pressure.

Rest

And perhaps most counterintuitive of all, excellent leaders rest—on purpose. They protect renewal the same way they protect deadlines. They understand that depleted leaders become reactive, and that reactive leaders unintentionally create reactive cultures. One executive told me, "If I don't rest, my burnout becomes my team's atmosphere." He treated rest as a responsibility rather than a reward.

All of these habits share one essential quality: repeatability. Excellence doesn't come from occasional heroic effort. It grows from ordinary behaviors practiced consistently enough that they become part of one's identity. Excellent leaders don't wait for motivation. They don't rely on adrenaline. They don't expect their best self to show up when needed. They trust the habits that shape them into the leader they intend to be.

One habit in my own life feels almost too simple to name, but it changed my leadership more than most formal training ever did. Every afternoon, before heading home, I take two minutes to write down three priorities for the next day. Just three. That small ritual quieted my 3 a.m. anxieties and gave each morning a place to begin. What I didn't expect was how much it shaped my team. When my priorities stabilized, their priorities did as well. My clarity created room for theirs.

A year later, when the organization introduced a formal list of recommended leadership practices, my team was already living most of them—not because I taught a class, but because my habits had quietly laid the foundation long before anyone named it.

Habits make excellence predictable. Predictable excellence builds trust. Trust multiplies results.

When people talk about excellent leaders years later, they rarely mention dramatic achievements. They remember steadiness. Groundedness. The sense that things were less chaotic simply because the leader was present.

Excellent leadership isn't charisma. It isn't brilliance. It isn't intensity. It's consistency—practiced quietly, reinforced daily, and carried faithfully over time.

That is the true habit of excellent leaders: they create a steadiness on which others can stand.

Chapter 14 – Creating a Culture of Excellence

Culture has a way of settling into every corner of an organization long before anyone fully realizes it's there. It behaves almost like the aroma inside our favorite coffee shop—the one that greets you the moment the door swings open. You can't touch it or quantify it, yet it shapes the entire experience. It influences how people speak to one another, how they respond to pressure, how they interpret expectations, and how they determine what matters.

The line often attributed to Peter Drucker is that culture eats strategy for breakfast, and I've always suspected that if strategy isn't careful, culture will return for lunch, dinner, and whatever snacks it can find in the breakroom. You can create the most elegant strategic plan imaginable—with charts, metrics, timelines, and a level of lamination impressive enough to survive a flood—but if the culture beneath it doesn't support excellence, the plan collapses under its own weight.

Culture is the unwritten rulebook of *how things really work around here*. It's not the framed values in the hallway, though those can be helpful reminders. Culture is the daily choreography of small choices—what leaders encourage, what they ignore, what they quietly bypass, and what they insist on protecting. It is the accumulation of the stories people tell about the organization when no one from leadership is present. Excellence doesn't become real because someone prints a slogan or unveils a new initiative. Excellence becomes real when people begin to notice the standard reflected in everyday actions and decide, "This is who we are."

Several years ago, at one of my outpatient surgery centers, the culture had become predictable. Mornings were frantic, afternoons were uneven, and the word *excellence* appeared more often in staff meetings than in the daily experience. This wasn't a team lacking commitment; they cared deeply about their patients and one another. But caring and consistency are not interchangeable, and when excellence lives only in aspiration rather than in habit, even good people can fall into patterns that undermine their own intentions.

One morning revealed this more clearly than any meeting ever could. A patient arrived for a minor procedure—a routine case, nothing urgent. When the surgeon reviewed the chart, however, he noted several missing elements: an incomplete medical history, an outdated medication list, and no preoperative clearance. None of it posed immediate danger, but the combined gaps delayed the case and sent frustration rippling through the team.

The surgeon felt irritated.

The pre-op nurse felt embarrassed.

The patient felt anxious and confused.

In that moment, the culture showed its true shape. The issue wasn't documentation; it was identity. Over time, the team had adopted an unspoken mantra: "We get it done eventually." It wasn't laziness—just drift. The slow erosion of a standard no one had actively chosen, but everyone had gradually accepted.

That day, the clinic administrator decided to interrupt the drift. She gathered the team, not with the sharpness of blame but with the steadiness of someone naming something important. Holding up the incomplete chart, she said calmly, "This isn't a paperwork problem. It's an identity problem. Excellence isn't something we check off. It's something we become."

And then she did something brave. She paused the entire pre-op workflow for 20 minutes.

Phones continued to ring. Patients kept arriving. The schedule tightened like a drawn string. In outpatient surgery, stopping the line feels almost sacrilegious. But she wasn't teaching efficiency in that moment; she was teaching identity. She was teaching the difference between moving fast and moving well.

With the workflow on hold, the team gathered around a dry-erase board and rebuilt their intake process from scratch. They clarified roles, established checkpoints, and defined what "complete" truly meant. She didn't dictate the system; she guided the team in creating it themselves, allowing them to take ownership not only of the task but also of its identity.

The shift that followed was not dramatic in the way sweeping changes often claim to be. It was something quieter, steadier, more rooted. Nurses began verifying documentation with renewed attentiveness. Medical assistants prepared charts the day before to eliminate surprises. Surgeons noticed the difference and matched the team's energy with their own steadier presence. Even patients felt the change and described the team as "organized," "confident," and "reassuring."

But the moment that confirmed the culture had truly shifted came a few weeks later, when a new hire shadowed her first morning. She watched the team move with coordinated ease and finally asked, "Who made this policy?"

A nurse smiled and said, "This isn't a policy. It's who we are now."

That sentence captures the essence of a culture of excellence. It isn't imposed. It isn't enforced through fear or pressure. It is embodied—so deeply rooted in daily behavior that it feels natural.

Not long after, I noticed something even smaller—so ordinary it would have been easy to miss. A supply cart was returned slightly out of order after a long, exhausting shift. No supervisor was nearby. No checklist demanded correction. A nurse passing by paused, straightened the cart without a word, and moved on. No announcement. No recognition. A quiet decision that said, "We leave things better than we found them." That moment never made it into a report, but it told me more about the culture than any survey ever could.

When leaders set out to build a culture of excellence, they're cultivating the intersection of three deeply human elements: shared purpose, shared standards, and shared accountability.

Shared Purpose — meaning people can feel

People don't rally around metrics; they rally around meaning. Purpose helps them understand not only what they're doing, but why it matters. Without purpose, excellence feels like compliance; with purpose, it becomes contribution. It turns effort into something with direction and significance.

Purpose turns work into service, and service into identity.

Shared Standards — clarity people can trust

Excellence cannot survive in ambiguity. When expectations are vague, "good enough" gradually becomes the most comfortable option. Shared standards transform ambiguity into alignment. When people understand what excellence looks like, when the standard is consistent and visible, they can move with confidence.

Clarity doesn't restrict people; it frees them from guessing.

Shared Accountability — ownership

Culture becomes real only when accountability is practiced at every level. When peers reinforce the standard with respect and leadership, that dynamic supports accountability, shifting it from a supervisory task to a shared commitment. Ownership becomes communal rather than positional. And when that happens, excellence becomes far easier to sustain because it no longer depends on a handful of leaders—it becomes the expectation everyone carries.

Most organizations broadcast their values through posters and slogans, but culture speaks in subtler ways. It shows up in how people respond when something goes wrong, how they treat newcomers, whether gratitude is common or rare, and how honestly they speak when stress levels rise. Humans learn culture not by instruction, but by imitation. Psychologists call this social proof. Most teams simply call it *how we do things here.*

The good news is that excellence spreads just as quickly as mediocrity. When someone goes above and beyond, and that action is recognized—even briefly—it sends a message about the team you are becoming. Recognition is not decoration. It is reinforcement—an internal compass pointing everyone toward the standard.

One of my leaders created a simple Shout-Out Wall in the breakroom—a corkboard where team members could pin handwritten notes acknowledging someone's help, compassion, creativity, or reliability. At first, the wall filled slowly, almost cautiously. But over time, it overflowed. They expanded it twice. People didn't participate to impress leadership; they participated because they were proud of what their teammates were becoming. Excellence had become visible, and visible excellence is contagious.

Cultures grow strong when three things happen consistently: Leaders model the behavior, teams mirror it, and recognition spreads it.

That cycle—modeling, mirroring, multiplying—becomes a flywheel. Once it gains momentum, culture becomes self-sustaining. Work ceases to feel like a collection of tasks and instead becomes a shared identity. Identity outlasts enthusiasm. It outlasts a crisis. It even outlasts leadership transitions.

Identity isn't abstract—it's shaped by language. Disney calls their staff "Cast Members." That single word turns work into a shared experience rather than a list of tasks.

A culture begins to slip when excellence is management's job, as if leaders hold the culture while everyone else observes it from the outside. Culture isn't something leaders create and hand off. It's something teams co-author. When people help define the culture, they naturally become its protectors.

That's why it's powerful to ask your team simple questions:

1. What do we do that makes you proud to work here?

2. What is something we should never compromise?

3. What small improvement would make us better this month?

Inviting people to define the culture is inviting them to own it.

So, if someone followed your team quietly for a week—no meetings, no presentations, no prepared explanations—what would they conclude you believe about excellence? Culture isn't shaped by what you say or celebrate once a year—it's shaped by what you tolerate and reinforce every day. Culture always answers that question honestly.

And like most meaningful things, culture grows through steady deposits—not grand gestures. It's built in the moments no one posts about: a teammate who resets the cart without being asked, a handoff done with care even when the shift is long, a quiet decision to tell the truth instead of protect an ego. Those moments are small, which is exactly why they shape the environment. They're repeatable.

That's where stories matter. Stories are how teams remember what "great" looks like when pressure rises and attention fades. If you don't name and repeat the right stories, the culture will still tell stories—just not the ones you want. Leaders don't create excellence by declaring it. They create it by reinforcing what they want repeated, in real time, until it becomes normal.

Excellence isn't an event, a slogan, or a line in a strategic plan. It's an environment—formed one decision at a time, one standard protected at a time, one moment of ownership at a time—until someone new steps into the room and senses it immediately: *This is who they are.*

And when that identity is reinforced consistently, culture stops being something you have to enforce.

It becomes something your people carry.

Chapter 15 – Excellence in Times of Challenge

It's easy to talk about excellence when the air is calm, the numbers are green, and the coffee machine is behaving like a loyal member of the team instead of blinking "ERROR" as if it has decided to resign mid-morning. Most people can nod along with high standards when circumstances feel generous. But the real measure of excellence isn't how we behave when everything is smooth. It's how we show up when the world begins to push back.

Excellence reveals its true character when life stops cooperating, when a deadline collapses like a soggy cardboard box. When a key supplier disappears at the worst possible moment. When the team is tired, customers are frustrated, tempers are thin, and your inbox looks like a crime scene. In those moments, excellence ceases to be an idea and becomes a decision.

Calm-water leadership is easy. Stormwater leadership is where character shows itself.

Storms eventually find every leader. Even healthy teams enter seasons where everything feels heavier, noisier, and less predictable than usual. But those seasons reveal something leaders often forget: excellence under pressure is not perfection. Its orientation. It's posture. It's the ability to stay anchored to what matters when the script falls apart.

Average leaders tighten their grip and try to control every variable. Excellent leaders tighten their principles and trust their people to think. Control says, "Do it exactly like I would." Principles say, "Here's what matters most—let's find a way forward." Control might carry you through the afternoon. Principles carry you through the crisis.

Several years ago, an outpatient primary care clinic I oversaw lost power during its busiest season. No lights. No air conditioning. No computers. No phones. The lobby was full; patients were already irritated by the delays, and the staff instinctively turned to the clinic director, waiting for the inevitable announcement that the day was over.

Instead, he stepped outside, scanned the parking lot, and said calmly, "We're not shutting down. We're shifting."

That sentence did more than announce a plan—it changed the emotional temperature of the room. Within minutes, exam tables were moved under shaded walkways. Nurses grabbed portable vitals carts. Medical assistants found blank paper for intake forms. Someone unearthed a stack of clipboards from a long-forgotten cabinet. A physician arrived amid the chaos and instinctively held umbrellas over two elderly patients while they waited. Nothing about the moment was rehearsed. There was no protocol for outdoor medicine (especially in Florida, in July!). No manual titled *Clinic Operations When Electricity Takes a Personal Day*. But excellence does not wait for ideal conditions.

Patients waiting in their cars cracked windows and listened for updates. A neighboring business observed the makeshift clinic forming and brought over shade tents without being asked. The staff moved with calm coordination rather than frantic improvisation. Even in the heat and inconvenience, the atmosphere felt steady. The purpose was to do the heavy lifting.

One older gentleman, after someone saw him under a canopy in the parking lot, said quietly, "I've never felt more cared for."

When the power company finally arrived hours later, they paused, visibly surprised to find a fully operational clinic running outside. The following month, patient satisfaction scores reached their highest level on record. Not because that day went smoothly, but because when everything else stopped working, the people didn't. That story became part of the clinic's identity. New hires heard it within their first week—not as a heroic legend, but as a simple statement of who the team was when it mattered.

Excellence isn't the absence of adversity. It's the willingness to remain yourself in the middle of it.

Under pressure, leaders often feel the urge to overfunction—do more, say more, grab tighter control, carry everything personally. But the teams that navigate storms well tend to ground themselves in three steady truths that remain intact even when everything else feels unstable: Purpose, Principles, and People.

1. **Purpose** becomes the anchor. It answers the question, "Why does this matter?" When circumstances wobble, purpose steadies the ground. It doesn't remove difficulty, but it restores direction, which is often enough to keep moving.

2. **Principles** become the compass. Plans can fail, but values don't have to. When the map tears,

principles still point north. They allow teams to improvise without losing integrity and to adapt without losing identity.

3. **People** remain the priority. Pressure tempts leaders to prioritize tasks over people, but those who feel seen and supported are far more capable of solving problems than those who feel rushed or dismissed. Care precedes coordination. A calm team solves problems a frantic team never will.

Teams don't need leaders pretending everything is fine. That overly cheerful "We've got this!" smile—the one leaders sometimes wear while silently negotiating with the universe for caffeine and mercy—fools no one. People don't need performance. They need presence. They need someone willing to acknowledge reality without surrendering to it.

There's science behind this. Under stress, the brain's alarm system becomes more pronounced, narrowing creativity and stiffening problem-solving. But humans also experience co-regulation—the way one person's steadiness helps settle another's nervous system. When a leader slows their breathing, lowers their shoulders, and speaks with measured clarity, they're not just leading emotionally.

They're helping the team regain access to the thinking required to move forward.

Panic spreads quickly, but so does steadiness.

To help leaders remember what grounded leadership looks like during disruption, I often offer a simple frame—not as a checklist, but as a reminder.

Communicate clearly. Share what you know, what you don't, and what comes next. Uncertainty multiplies in silence.

Adapt quickly. Adjust tactics, not values. Flexibility is strength. Inconsistency is not.

Lead visibly. Be present. Crises magnify absence. People draw confidence from proximity.

Maintain standards. Stress doesn't excuse sloppiness. Excellence may look different under pressure, but it still matters.

Something to note: calm leadership is not passive leadership. It's not detached or indecisive. It's the deliberate choice to be a stabilizing presence when instability feels inevitable.

For many years, I travelled extremely frequently for my role (yes, the acknowledgments to my wife and kids are very real – they are the real heroes). When you travel a lot, you notice many things during your time in airports. I once observed a gate agent do this effectively during a major weather delay. Dozens of flights were canceled, frustration hung in the air like static, and travelers braced for conflict. She picked up the microphone and said, "We know this is frustrating. We're stuck too. But we're going to stay with you and do everything we can. Come up one at a time, and we'll help you." 20 seconds of honest, steady communication softened the tension of a hundred exhausted people. Excellence doesn't always require resources. Often, it requires tone.

In seasons of pressure, excellence is not about operating at full capacity. It's about offering the best available version of yourself. On some days, that version is strong and energized. On other days, it is simply steady and present. If you normally operate at 100 percent but today all you can offer is 80 percent, that 80 percent—delivered with clarity and calm—is far more valuable than panic-driven heroics.

NASA's Apollo 13 mission captured this truth on a historic scale. When an oxygen tank exploded in space, the now-famous phrase "Failure is not an option" wasn't a demand for perfection. It was a declaration of determination. Engineers improvised with limited tools, invented procedures mid-flight, and brought the crew home safely. Excellence wasn't the absence of failure. It was the refusal to abandon the mission despite the plan's collapse.

What many leaders miss is that every crisis plants seeds for future culture. Disruption can become development if you're willing to pause afterward and learn from it. After the pressure passes, ask your team simple questions:

What worked?

What didn't?

What should we do differently next time?

Don't waste the difficulty. Turn it into wisdom. Let it refine your assumptions, your habits, and your systems.

Excellence isn't proven in easy seasons. It is revealed, shaped, and strengthened in the difficult ones. Every blackout, setback, conflict, or crisis becomes a paragraph in the story your organization tells about who it is when things get hard.

Ultimately, that story matters more than any polished plan.

Chapter 16 – Sustaining Excellence Over Time

Organizations love beginnings. They love ribbon-cuttings, kickoff meetings, and fresh initiatives wrapped in color-coded slide decks. Something is intoxicating about that clean start—the sense that this time, everything will run smoother, faster, smarter. Beginnings spark hope. They make people lean in. They prompt leaders to imagine climbing the mountain ahead in a single, inspiring montage set to upbeat music, with no setbacks.

But sustaining excellence?

That is where reality begins to assert itself.

Peaks are thrilling, but they're also temporary. You can stand on a summit for a moment, but you cannot live there. Eventually, the air thins, the wind stiffens, and gravity becomes very apparent. Excellence works in much the same way. It isn't a moment or a medal; it's a rhythm—a long, steady pattern of climbing, resting, recalibrating, and climbing again.

Even the strongest teams eventually feel the strain. It's not a flaw—it's physiology. After a prolonged stretch of elevated performance, people hit a silent wall. Focus blurs. Mistakes slip through cracks. Meetings feel heavier. Small annoyances expand into disproportionate frustrations. This isn't laziness or disengagement; it's the predictable consequence of running too long on momentum without renewal.

The truth is as simple as it is unavoidable:

Excellence cannot exist without recovery.

If leaders want excellence that lasts, they have to guide their teams—and themselves—into a leadership breathing pattern:

Push → Pause → Reflect → Refocus.

The pause isn't a sign that excellence is fading. The pause is what sustains excellence.

A few years back, I worked for a rapidly expanding outpatient organization—new clinics opening, patient volume soaring, staffing teams racing to keep up, news outlets calling us "the future of healthcare." From the outside, we looked unstoppable.

On the inside, it felt like sprinting through mud.

Leaders were working 12-hour days. Front-line teams were stretched to capacity. PTO became something people apologized for (we called it **P**retend **T**ime **O**ff). The mission that had once energized the entire company now felt like a weight strapped to everyone's back.

And then the moment came—the one that broke the surface.

During a quarterly leadership meeting, a manager who had always been the steady one—the anchor you count on when things get complicated—paused mid-presentation. She took a breath, tried to continue, and then whispered through tears she'd been holding back for months:

"I love this place... but I'm losing myself."

The room fell silent. Not because she'd said something inappropriate, but because she had spoken aloud a truth that every person in the room had felt in their bones but hadn't dared to articulate.

I didn't respond with a polished leadership speech. I didn't offer a motivational metaphor or remind the room that "pressure builds diamonds." Instead, I closed my laptop gently, looked around the table, and with an honesty that softened every shoulder in the room, said something like:

"If excellence costs people their health, their families, or their joy, then it isn't excellence."

Then I made a decision no one expected (I shocked myself a bit, too, if I'm being honest).

I paused all new initiatives for 30 days, knowing I would get slack for it later (this is certainly not something you do in a region turnaround situation).

In a world obsessed with perpetual motion, a pause feels like an act of rebellion. Boards don't love it. Investors don't celebrate it. Hypergrowth strategies don't accommodate it. But I wasn't protecting growth at that moment; I was protecting the people responsible for it.

During that 30-day pause, several meaningful shifts unfolded:

Meeting footprints were cut in half.

Clinics received floating support staff.

Leaders gave teams protected time to train, breathe, regroup, and strengthen workflows.

Leaders were told explicitly, "If you're still here at 6 p.m., you're modeling the wrong thing."

No fireworks. No dramatic overhaul. Just space—something the region didn't even realize it had been starving for.

And here is the twist: the region didn't lose speed. It gained strength (thankfully, for my career's sake).

When we resumed, teams didn't limp forward—they stood taller. Creativity resurfaced. Collaboration felt easier again. Pride returned. And in the months that followed, turnover—quietly creeping upward before the pause—began to move back down. The essential KPIs began trending in a positive direction. We were building momentum.

Later, someone asked me why I made such a risky call at the height of the organization's momentum. I smiled and said something like:

"Excellence isn't something you squeeze out of people. It's something that flows from healthy, whole, energized teams."

And that, more than any initiative or strategy, is the heart of sustained excellence.

There is a simple equation behind it—one that leaders often nod along to but rarely operationalize:

Sustained Excellence = Purpose + Pace + People

- **Purpose** keeps the work meaningful

- **Pace** keeps it human

- **People** keep it alive.

You can fake excellence for a quarter—even a year—but no one can fake it for an entire career.

My college baseball coach once told me, "We practice hard six days a week, but on the seventh, I make you rest." When I asked why, he answered in a way that lodged itself into my leadership vocabulary:

"Because tired players learn bad habits."

I've never forgotten that line. Tired leaders do, too.

Fatigue doesn't just drain energy; it warps judgment. It shrinks patience. It narrows creativity. A tired leader is more irritable, more anxious, more easily overwhelmed, and more likely to misinterpret people or problems. Rest isn't indulgence; rest is infrastructure. It protects clarity, emotional steadiness, and wise decision-making—three things excellence cannot exist without.

Leaders who sustain excellence over the long haul tend to anchor themselves in three quiet but powerful patterns:

1. Renewal

Sleep, movement, breathing room, stillness. Not leftover margin scraped from the corners of the calendar, but intentional rest woven into the rhythm of a life.

2. Reflection

The willingness to learn from what worked, what didn't, and what changed. Reflection transforms experience into wisdom.

3. Relationships

Staying connected to people who speak truth offers grounding and reminds you who you are when stress tries to make you forget.

Some organizations embed these patterns so naturally that you almost don't notice them. Patagonia encourages employees to surf when the waves are good or head outdoors when the day is too perfect to waste. That flexibility doesn't create slackers. It creates loyal, energized, high-performing people who return with more clarity than when they left.

Contrast that with the leader who sends a Saturday-night email at 11 p.m. titled "Not urgent!"—a contradiction so obvious the entire team groans. If it weren't urgent, it could wait until Monday. People don't believe what leaders *say* about rest; they believe what leaders *model* about rest.

Sustained excellence requires rhythm, and the healthiest teams openly acknowledge it. They build it into the way they work:

__Rhythm__	__Practice__	__Frequency__
Daily Reset	10–15 minutes of quiet, breathing, or centering review	Daily
Weekly Recharge	Protected rest or intentional unplugging	Weekly
Quarterly Review	Revisit goals, progress, and lessons learned	Quarterly
Annual Retreat	Fully unplug—no email, no meetings, no agenda	Yearly

These rhythms are not perks. They are the maintenance schedule for excellence (and frankly, for life).

But even with healthy rhythms, strong teams face another temptation—the slow drift that follows success. After a big win, it becomes easy to shift from intentionality to autopilot, not out of arrogance, but out of comfort. Familiarity replaces curiosity. Momentum replaces discipline. Unfortunately, drift doesn't announce itself; it settles in quietly.

Teams who want to sustain excellence resist that drift by running a simple quarterly diagnostic I call the Excellence Pulse Check:

Clarity: Do we still know what "great" looks like?

- **Energy:** Are we fueled or depleted?

- **Learning:** Are we improving or repeating?

You are not looking for perfection; you are looking for truth—truth you can act on.

All too many times, I'm sure you have heard a well-intentioned leader tell their exhausted team, "Next year, we're going to start strong and stay strong!" The room didn't lift. It deflated. They didn't need more intensity—they needed recovery and margin.

Motivation can spark excellence, yes, but carving out and wisely using margin sustains it.

Because excellence is not something you ignite once and admire indefinitely. It's something you tend to. Something you protect. Something you feed with purpose, pace, and people.

You don't sustain excellence by squeezing harder. You sustain it by leading wiser.

Chapter 17 – The Legacy of Reframed Leadership

If you really want to understand a leader—who they are, what they build, what they truly believe—you don't watch them in the spotlight. You watch what happens when they leave the room. Not immediately, when people are still nodding out of professional habit, but 10 minutes later, when the conversation settles back into its natural rhythm. Does the room stall, and are you unsure about which decisions are permitted without supervision? Does the energy dip as people wait for the "real boss" to return? Or does the team keep moving—thinking, adapting, solving— because you equipped them to lead, not simply comply?

Here's the question that cuts through every illusion of leadership:

After you're gone, do results continue—or does everything revert?

Your real legacy isn't measured by the activity that happens in your presence. It's measured by the capability that continues in your absence. Legacy isn't performance. It's what you leave others able to do without you.

People often define leadership by achievements—what you built, what you improved, what you can point to on a dashboard or tuck into an annual report. Those things matter, but they don't endure. Buildings get remodeled. Strategies get replaced. Programs expire. Titles have a shelf life only slightly longer than bananas. But people carry forward the parts of you that can't be archived. Legacy isn't measured in moments; it's measured in multiplication. It's not whether you were great. It's whether your greatness became contagious.

I saw this truth play out at a celebration for a director who was being promoted and leaving his center—we'll call him Tom. The room was staged the way organizations love to stage success: glossy posters of achievements and awards. It was packed with people he'd personally hired and developed over the years. It looked exactly like what most companies celebrate when someone moves up.

Then Tom walked to the front of the room, glanced at the posters, and deliberately stood several feet away from them. Instead, he invited three people forward. The first had once been his first front-desk receptionist. The second started years earlier as an entry-level sales rep. The third had come in as the clinic janitor.

Tom placed a hand on each of their shoulders and said, "These are the metrics that matter."

The room shifted—not loudly, not dramatically, but with the stillness that signals truth arriving. He said something like: "Buildings will be renovated. New systems will replace the old ones. Numbers will rise and fall," pausing long enough for the words to land. "But people carry your work into places you'll never step."

And they did! The former receptionist was eventually promoted to operations manager. The entry-level sales rep went on to become VP of National Sales at a much larger organization. And the janitor—quiet, steady, never needing the spotlight—was later promoted to Lead Culture Ambassador, because everyone knew culture was already in his hands.

After the celebration, while people hugged and wiped their eyes, a younger team member pulled Tom aside and asked what he was most proud of. She expected him to point to the trophies or the charts. Instead, he nodded toward the three leaders still surrounded by colleagues. "I didn't just run a clinic," he said quietly. "I built leaders who can run it better than I ever could."

That is the heart of legacy. Not your résumé—your ripple.

Legacy is less like a monument and more like muscle memory. It's the way people continue to show up, not because you're watching, but because that's who they became under your leadership.

If you want a simple framework for understanding legacy, you can think of it like this:

Legacy = People × Principles × Time

The people you influence.

The principles you model clearly and consistently enough for others to adopt.

The time required for those lessons to outlive your presence.

If you lead through that lens, your name may fade, but your impact won't.

A young leader once told me about his former leader, Martha, with a tenderness you don't usually hear in corporate settings. "She never made it about her," he said. "She taught me how to think, not what to think. Even now,

I can hear her voice asking, 'Does that serve the purpose?' every time I face a decision." That's legacy—the echo that shapes decisions long after your voice is no longer in the hallway.

Psychologists call this generativity: the impulse to develop the next generation, to invest in people who will carry your influence into a future you won't fully see. Some leaders climb ladders. Others build ladders. The second group creates lineage.

A useful way to reflect on your own legacy is through what I call the Three-Generation Reflection:

1. **Who invested in me?** (Gratitude.)

2. **Who am I investing in now?** (Responsibility.)

3. **Who will those people invest in next?** (Legacy.)

If you can name all three, you are already leading beyond your own lifetime.

I once heard an executive engineer say, "Everything I ever built started in Mrs. Thompson's ninth-grade science class. She saw something in me before I did." A single sentence from a teacher led this engineer to achieve over three decades of innovation that literally changed the world, seven U.S. Patents, and a legacy that continues to this day—even outside his career, because that engineer was my dad, my hero. And Mrs. Thompson, the seed planter, never knew any of this. That is legacy's reach: influence expanding across years and landscapes the leader never fully saw or realized.

Organizations that understand this build generativity into their DNA. Pixar doesn't just make films—they make filmmakers. Senior animators mentor new ones. Directors develop future directors. Excellence doesn't endure because the original team was brilliant; it endures because brilliance was passed on deliberately.

Reframed leadership follows the same blueprint.

You can think of legacy as a lighthouse. A lighthouse doesn't chase ships or sprint along the shoreline. It stands steady, shines clearly, and offers guidance without demanding control. A lighthouse is most useful when the light guides ships—even if no one knows who's tending it. That is legacy—influence without insistence.

You can even map this progression visually:

> **Rung 1:** Dependence — results run through you (you're the bottleneck).

Rung 2: Ownership — results run through them (you built clarity, trust, and autonomy).

Rung 3: Multiplication — leaders run through them (they invest and empower others).

Most leaders climb the first rung. Many reach the second. Very few reach the third—the place where influence becomes culture rather than a skill set. But invested leaders do. And then they build more ladders.

There's an old proverb that says, "A society grows great when old men plant trees whose shade they know they will never sit in." Leadership is no different. People measure your legacy by the shade you will never rest under—the people who thrive because you invested early, believed deeply, and released control at exactly the right time.

Ultimately, your leadership will not be remembered by what you controlled, but by what you entrusted to others. Not by what you built with your own hands, but by what you equipped others to build with theirs. Not by how brightly you shone, but by how many lights you ignited.

As people grow, excellence becomes normal—and legacy follows.

And that is the long shadow of your reframed leadership—a legacy that outlasts every title, every season, every chapter… and most importantly, outlasts you.

Operating Notes — Put This into Practice

This week, make excellence durable and legacy real—install the rhythms and reinforcements that hold when you're not in the room.

Actions

- Name the real standard: pick one "this is who we are" behavior and protect it in the small moments (not in slogans).

- Install one repeatable habit: end each day with a two-minute check: "What worked? What didn't? What matters next?"

- Set tomorrow's three priorities: write them before you leave—then start the next day with clarity instead of reaction.

- Practice specific gratitude: thank one person for something concrete you want repeated.

- Build recovery into excellence: schedule a pause—even a short one—so the team can breathe, regroup, and strengthen workflows.

- When pressure hits, tighten principles—not control: state purpose, name what matters most, and trust people to think.

Scripts (use them verbatim if you want)

1. **Steady in the storm**

   "Alright. Let's figure this out. Here's what matters most right now. We'll stay anchored and move."

2. **Push → Pause → Reflect → Refocus**

   "We're going to pause on purpose. What did we learn, and what needs to change? Then we refocus and go again."

Watch-fors

- Perfection masquerading as excellence: people brace, hide mistakes, and stop learning in public.

- Urgency as identity: living on adrenaline until recovery becomes "optional."

- Culture talk without culture practice: laminated strategy, but the daily choreography stays the same.

Reflection questions

- What does my team mirror from me when things get tense—panic or steadiness?

- Where do we need a pause so strength can return?

- If excellence is "the next right thing, repeated," what is our next right thing this week?

Conclusion

What's Your Next Step?

If we were back in that same coffee shop where this journey began—just you, me, our predictable orders, and the quiet hum of conversation—I imagine I'd let the silence sit for a moment before asking the one question that matters now more than anything we've covered:

"So… what's your next step?"

Not your next meeting. Not the task waiting in your inbox. Not the email thread that refuses to die.

Your next leadership step.

The one that requires courage instead of convenience. Intention instead of instinct. Because reading about leadership is the easy part, living it—choosing it repeatedly—comes at a cost. It requires time, trust, vulnerability, and a willingness to grow publicly. But the fact that you've made it to the end of these pages tells me something important:

You're willing to invest.

And if you're willing, you're already farther along than most.

Before we close our tab and step back into the noise of the world, it's worth glancing over our shoulder at the road we've walked together.

- You saw that leadership begins with investment—the steady kind, poured into people rather than splashed when it's convenient.

- You explored empowerment not as a buzzword, but as a belief in someone's capacity, even before they fully recognize it themselves.

- You wrestled with autonomy—not as chaos, but as clarity paired with freedom.

- You reframed excellence away from perfection and toward consistency, intention, and progress.

And along the way, whether you noticed it or not, you began shaping something bigger than your role:

A legacy built not on accomplishments, but on people.

That isn't management or technique.

That is stewardship.

A mentor once told me, "You'll never know how far your influence travels—but you'll feel the ripples if you keep throwing stones." Influence rarely announces itself. It moves quietly, through a shift in someone's confidence, the steadiness of a team, or the moment a leader chooses courage over control because of something they learned from you.

Every time you choose curiosity over certainty, trust over grip, development over dismissal, you drop another stone into the water. And somewhere—maybe tomorrow, maybe years from now—someone who you may never meet will lead differently because of a moment that began with you.

That's the power of reframed leadership.

One of the great myths leaders eventually have to let go of is the idea of arriving—the belief that someday you'll finally "get it," feel finished, or lead without uncertainty. But leadership doesn't work that way. There is no destination. There is only the next step, taken with purpose.

If you need something to orient you as you move forward, you don't need a complex framework. You need a direction:

- Invest deeply.

- Empower wisely.

- Trust freely.

- Pursue excellence steadily.

You won't always have the full map, but with those in hand, you won't lose your way.

And on the most ordinary days—the Tuesday mornings filled with meetings, lukewarm coffee, and fatigue—leadership often shows up in small, faithful deposits:

- A few minutes of listening to understand without distraction.

- A word of encouragement offered at the right moment.

- A responsibility is released because someone is ready—an intentional investment in someone's growth.

These moments rarely feel dramatic. But repeated over time, they shape cultures faster than any initiative ever will.

As you move forward, hold onto this truth: your leadership will only grow as far as you're willing to grow.

So, stay curious. Seek feedback. Learn from people who will tell you the truth with care. The best leaders aren't the ones who get it right—they're the ones who keep getting better.

If everything else from this book fades with time, I hope one conviction remains:

Leadership is never about you becoming the hero. It's about helping others become strong enough to stand on their own.

That is the heart of the Invested Leadership platform.

Leaders exist to invest and empower others to be autonomously excellent.

You invest so people can rise without you. You develop so others can lead beyond you.

And one day, they'll invest in others the way you invested in them.

So, finish your coffee. Gather your things. Step back into the world you influence far more than you realize.

Because the world doesn't need more bosses. It needs more Invested Leaders.

It needs you.

References

Catmull, E., & Wallace, A. (2014). Creativity, Inc.: Overcoming the unseen forces that stand in the way of true inspiration. Random House.

Chouinard, Y. (2005). Let my people go surfing: The education of a reluctant businessman. Penguin Books.

Cialdini, R. B. (2009). Influence: Science and practice (5th ed.). Pearson.

Drucker, P. F. (2006). The effective executive: The definitive guide to getting the right things done. HarperBusiness.

Edmondson, A. C. (1999). Psychological safety and learning behavior in work teams. Administrative Science Quarterly, 44(2), 350–383. https://doi.org/10.2307/2666999

Edmondson, A. C. (2018). The fearless organization: Creating psychological safety in the workplace for learning, innovation, and growth. Wiley.

Google. (n.d.). Guide: Understand team effectiveness (Project Aristotle). re:Work with Google. Retrieved January 14, 2026, from https://rework.withgoogle.com/guides/under-standing-team-effectiveness/steps/introduction/

Kranz, G. (2000). Failure is not an option: Mission control from Mercury to Apollo 13 and beyond. Simon & Schuster.

Pierce, J. L., Kostova, T., & Dirks, K. T. (2001). Toward a theory of psychological ownership in organizations. Academy of Management Review, 26(2), 298–310.
https://doi.org/10.5465/AMR.2001.4378028

Prokesch, S. E. (2008, August 19). Pixar's collective genius. Harvard Business Review. Retrieved January 14, 2026, from https://hbr.org/2008/08/pixars-collective-genius

Quote Investigator. (2017, May 23). Quote origin: Culture eats strategy for breakfast. Retrieved January 14, 2026, from https://quoteinvestigator.com/2017/05/23/culture-eats/

Rozovsky, J. (2015, November 17). The five keys to a successful Google team. re:Work with Google. Retrieved January 14, 2026, from https://rework.withgoogle.com/blog/five-keys-to-a-successful-google-team/

Safian, R. (2025, October 15). Airbnb CEO Brian Chesky breaks down the difference between a business decision and a principle decision. Fast Company. Retrieved January 14, 2026, from https://www.fastcompany.com/91201001/airbnb-ceo-brian-chesky-breaks-down-the-difference-between-a-business-decision-and-a-principle-decision

Thaler, R. H., & Sunstein, C. R. (2008). Nudge: Improving decisions about health, wealth, and happiness. Yale University Press.

The Walt Disney Company / Disney Institute. (n.d.). Disney customer service 101: Why courtesy is not always our first priority. Disney Institute Blog. Retrieved January 14, 2026, from https://www.disneyinstitute.com/blog/disney-customer-service-101-why-courtesy-is-not-always-our-first-priority/

Patel, N. (2024, October 28). Airbnb CEO Brian Chesky on the gospel of Steve Jobs and what founder mode really means. The Verge. Retrieved January 14, 2026, from https://www.theverge.com/24279570/airbnb-ceo-brian-chesky-founder-mode-apple-steve-jobs-management-decoder-podcast-2024

IF YOU NEED SUPPORT

If you or someone you love is struggling, you don't have to carry it alone.

- **United States:** Call or text **988** (988 Suicide & Crisis Lifeline). You can also chat through the 988 Lifeline website.

- **Canada:** Call or text **9-8-8** (Suicide Crisis Helpline).

- **United Kingdom & Ireland:** Call **116 123** (Samaritans).

- **Australia:** Call **13 11 14** (Lifeline).

If you're in immediate danger or need urgent help, call your local emergency number.

Attributions

Drucker / "Culture eats strategy for breakfast" — Widely circulated leadership aphorism is often attributed to Peter Drucker; attribution and origin are disputed in published quote research (see References).

Psychological safety — Research and concept attributed to Amy C. Edmondson (see References).

Google / Project Aristotle — Team effectiveness findings and the "five dynamics" summary referenced via Google's re:Work materials (see References).

Decision Architecture — Term used in behavioral economics and choice design; referenced as a leadership application (see Thaler & Sunstein in References).

Social proof — Behavioral influence concept referenced as a leadership dynamic (see Cialdini in References).

Psychological ownership — Concept referenced as a driver of "mine/ours" thinking at work (see Pierce, Kostova, & Dirks in References).

Airbnb — Referenced as an illustrative example of scaling clarity and decision-making at speed; supporting leadership/decision-making discussions drawn from published interviews/articles (see References).

Pixar — Referenced as an illustrative example of development culture ("make filmmakers"); supporting discussion drawn from published accounts of Pixar's creative/learning culture (see References).

Disney — "Cast Members" terminology and service-standards decision guidance referenced via Disney Institute materials (see References).

Patagonia — Referenced as an illustrative example of culture practices aligned to values (see References).

NASA / Apollo 13 / "Failure is not an option" — Referenced as an illustrative leadership story and widely popularized phrase; mission-control perspective reflected in published accounts (see References).

About the Author

Michael A. Bruggeman has spent more than two decades serving in executive leadership roles in high-stakes healthcare, leading many teams through real pressures that don't show up in leadership theory: limited resources, urgent decisions, competing priorities, and the human weight leaders carry when the work truly matters.

His leadership foundation was also shaped outside the corporate world, where he spent ten years serving as a pastor, forming a people-first lens that blends clarity with compassion and accountability with care. That combination—results and humanity—sits at the center of the Invested Leadership platform.

Michael's academic path reflects the same integration. He holds three master's degrees: an MBA, a Master of Divinity, and a Master of Organizational Leadership— bringing together strategy, purpose, and practical systems for developing people who can think, decide, and own outcomes.

Michael lives in Central Florida with his wife, Kristin, and is the proud father of two grown children. Outside of work, you'll find him cooking for friends and family, riding his motorcycles, and creating music.

If this book helped you, Michael would love to hear from you and continue the conversation.

To connect and for additional resources, go to:

Website: www.investedleadership.org